COMPETENT LEADERSHIP

Presenting the Knowledge to Lead,
along with the Practical Lessons
and Experience to Do It Well

T. S. (Steve) Marshall, Ph.D.

authorHOUSE®

AuthorHouse™
1663 Liberty Drive
Bloomington, IN 47403
www.authorhouse.com
Phone: 1 (800) 839-8640

Published by AuthorHouse 08/02/2018

ISBN: 978-1-5462-5377-8 (sc)
ISBN: 978-1-5462-5376-1 (e)

CONTENTS

FOREWORD

As a businessperson and educator, I have spent the past two decades helping emerging and established leaders to develop professionally and succeed at work and life. *This book is about the knowledge to lead along with the practical lessons and experience to do it well.* Though not a workbook, there are plenty of opportunities in this book to assess, examine, and develop your leadership and the environments (at work, home, and elsewhere) within which it occurs. Along the way, I hope you will pause your read long enough to reflect on the leadership lessons as they relate to you.

My leadership expertise is grounded in business, education, and life. I was a police officer at age 19, led a multi-national company of 50+ people at age 25, and later managed operations of a 2,000+ organization. During that time, I earned my undergraduate, graduate, and doctorate degrees in management and leadership. Since then, I have taught in the business program as fulltime faculty at the University of Washington-Tacoma, and for the past nine years I have taught in the Master of Public Administration Program at The Evergreen State College as adjunct faculty.

I left fulltime faculty to develop and lead a firm that provides leadership and professional development training, consulting, and coaching to national and multi-national organizations, higher education, healthcare, and federal, state, and local agencies in the U.S., Australia, England, Hong Kong, India, Indonesia, Philippines, Korea, Poland, and Singapore. Domestic and foreign travel, multicultural experiences, and personal relationships with people of many nationalities have resulted in an immense understanding and appreciation for leadership in varied cultures and organizational contexts. Regarding business and leadership: I have a proven record of accomplishment in knowing it, doing it, and teaching it.

Just like there is no one-style-fits-all approach to leadership, reliance on only one book, one voice, one approach is ill advised. *Want to become a better leader?* Read whatever you can on leadership, learn what you can, and practice, practice, practice. Bear in mind, leadership does not discriminate: a formal position or title does not make someone a leader, and a leader may not have a formal position or title. One does not necessarily come with the other.

ACKNOWLEDGEMENTS

I wish to thank my wife, Sandra, and adult children, Justin and Morgen, who offered comments on early drafts and patiently supported me during the writing of this book. Their insights were always welcomed and immensely valuable.

Also, I would like to express my deepest gratitude to two of my business colleagues, Maria Luisa T. Acosta, J.D.; and Brian J. Peters, Ed.D., whose leadership knowledge and experience have benefited me tremendously over the years. Thank you both.

Finally, many thanks to those who were the first to review my manuscript in whole or in part: Thomas M. Cioppa, Ph.D.; Richard W. Stackman, Ph.D.; Alannah Bjur, RN, MS; and Kelly S. Johnston. They provided their professional perspectives and intellectual insights that helped me finish this important work.

CHAPTER 1

WHAT IS LEADERSHIP

Don and Sue were alike in many ways: both had like seniority and held the same position as Regional Director in the same regional office (at different times) under the same CEO. Though they had much in common, they could not be more different.

DON CAME FIRST. In his mind, he was a gift to his staff. Though the organization had a mission, the job of the staff—comprised mostly of professional and technical staff—was to make him look good and get him promoted. He made this perfectly clear. Since he was the Director, Don believed his leadership, by default of title and position, was implicit and not to be questioned. He made most of the decisions and told his staff what to do, when to do it, and how to do it. Ever confident, Don even told his staff that if they were successful, one day, they could be just like him. Don's style suffocated the staff, and morale plummeted; people reluctantly came to work and were eager to leave at the end of the day. In the end, Don was reassigned to another position within the region—not the big promotion he hoped for, but he was out of the picture.

THEN CAME SUE. The difference in styles astounded the staff. Sue clarified the organization's mission, shared responsibilities, asked the staff to participate in problem solving and decision making, and reassured and supported them in achieving personal and organizational outcomes. Who is this person, they wondered. Sue mentored staff, recognized and rewarded contributions, and, essentially, got out of their way so they could do the

1

job they always wanted to do. She fostered a sense of purpose, autonomy, and mastery. Under her leadership, organizational performance, customer satisfaction, and morale flourished. People could not wait to come to work. For the first time in a long while, staff had brown-bag lunches to discuss improvement ideas and even hung around at the end of the day to tie up loose ends. It was not long before executive leadership recognized her talents and whisked her away. Sue got the big promotion that Don hoped for.

Sue's promotion made her Don's supervisor, a cruel irony for Don. He could not believe it. In his mind, Sue did not do anything. When he was Director, he was busy all the time "directing"—what, in his thinking, directors are supposed to do—and driving numbers (performance). I bet you think this story is fiction; I wish it were.

Like the story of Don and Sue, people generally know leadership when they see it, but putting what they see into words can be challenging. Knowing what makes a leader is important because *to become better* at anything, you need to know *what to get better at*—what specifically must you know and do? To Don, leadership came with the position; it meant being directive: telling people what, when, and how to do their jobs. To Sue, leadership was a process; it meant enabling people to be successful and then getting out of their way.

What is heartbreaking is Don was probably a good person. Regrettably, he never learned or was taught how to be a leader. In the absence of knowing, Don did what he thought leaders do; unfortunately, he was wrong. Sue, on the other hand, was a gifted leader. She clarified direction and purpose, and listened to and supported her staff. A good description of leadership suited to this story is: "As for the best leaders, the people do not notice their existence. The next best, the people honor and praise. The next, the people fear. The next, the people hate" (Lao Tse, 604-531 b.c.).

Leadership applies to everyone, everywhere. Whether a formal or informal leader, at work or at home, we all have to do it. It is not always planned, but when it happens, inevitably, someone has to step up. So, learning important leadership skills can only help. There is no downside. The good news: *leadership skills and competencies are mostly learned.* Whatever your leadership abilities or behaviors are now, it is good to know they can get better. In this chapter, we will explore the definition of leadership, types of leaders, influence, reputation, and an approach for developing leadership behaviors.

Here are a few of my favorite quotations that describe leadership and leader behaviors:

- ➤ The first job of a leader is to define a vision for the organization… Leadership is the capacity to translate vision into reality. (Warren Bennis)
- ➤ If there is anything I would like to be remembered for it is that I helped people understand that leadership is helping other people grow and succeed. To repeat myself, leadership is not just about you. It's about them. (Jack Welch)
- ➤ A genuine leader is not a searcher for consensus but a molder of consensus. (Martin Luther King, Jr.)
- ➤ If your actions inspire others to dream more, learn more, do more and become more, you are a leader. (John Quincy Adams)
- ➤ A manager takes people where they want to go. A great leader takes people where they don't necessarily want to go but ought to. (Rosalyn Carter)
- ➤ [A] leader…is a [person] who can persuade people to do what they don't want to do, or do what they're too lazy to do, and like it. (Harry S. Truman)
- ➤ Great leaders are almost always great simplifiers, who can cut through argument, debate and doubt, to offer a solution everybody can understand. (Colin Powell)
- ➤ …acts by persons which influence other persons in a shared direction. (Seeman, 1960)
- ➤ In the past a leader was a boss. Today's leaders must be partners with their people; they no longer can lead solely based on positional power. (Ken Blanchard)

Which quotation best defines your understanding of leadership? What themes resonate with you? Though many definitions of *leadership* exist, the following seems to sum it up.

> *Leadership* is the process of influencing others to pursue a shared goal. *Leaders* do not move people; they influence movement.

To know something—like *what is leadership*—we not only need to *recognize* the presence (or absence) of it, but we must also *know* what constitutes it. It is much like a delicious meal: many will know it tastes amazing, but few will have an understanding of the ingredients and the know-how to recreate it. The latter is crucial to becoming a leader. To become a leader, we need to have an understanding of leadership practices, approaches, and competencies—the leadership ingredients—and the know-how to appropriately use them and to lead authentically.

Consider today's environments (at work, home, or elsewhere): what do people *want* and *don't want* from their leaders? I have been asking people in government, business, education, and healthcare this question for more than a decade, and responses are remarkably consistent. Common responses are:

What people *want* from their leaders:

➢ Respect	➢ Professionalism	➢ Not taking things personal
➢ Appreciation	➢ Feedback; Participation	➢ Doing their share of work
➢ Support	➢ Ability to ask questions	➢ Ability to make a decision
➢ Fairness	➢ Open-mindedness	
➢ Confidence	➢ Good communication	
➢ Cooperation	➢ Trustworthy, Honest	

What people *don't want* from their leaders:

➢ Bullying	➢ Unprofessionalism	➢ Being set in their ways
➢ Micromanaging	➢ Incompetence	➢ Dishonesty
➢ Double talk	➢ Credit grabbing	➢ Arrogance
➢ Favoritism	➢ Complacency	➢ Manipulator
➢ Shaming	➢ Intimidation	➢ Being indecisive

The above words are not unique to leaders or leadership; for example, both groups of responses can apply to managers, executives, colleagues, friends, partners, spouses, and people in general. Implicit in both lists is an understanding that the behaviors of outstanding leaders are those of outstanding people too. Even so, it is interesting that a broad group of people across sectors and organizational levels use similar words to describe what they *want* and *don't want* from their leaders. I bet you can add a few of your own responses to each of the above questions.

So, to understand leadership, it is important to know it when you see it, as well as when you do not (see Figure 1.1). For instance, I would contend that many of the words above that describe what people *don't want from their leaders* are not the result of leadership at all; bullying, threats, and micromanaging is **not** leadership. Granted, the person exhibiting such behavior(s) may occupy a *leadership position*, but titles and position do **not** make someone a leader—a manager or executive perhaps, but a leader? No.

Figure 1.1: <u>Leadership: Recognize the Presence (or Absence) of It</u>

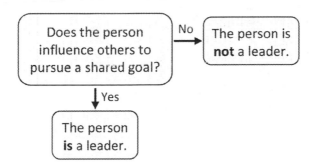

Moreover, not being a leader does not make someone a bad leader; you cannot be bad at what does not exist. For example, you cannot be a *bad driver* if you *do not drive*; you cannot be a *bad spouse* if you are *not married*. So, do not confuse the *absence of leadership* with *bad leadership*. If a person lacks the desire and/or ability to lead, then they are **not** a leader, period. There is nothing to qualify. Furthermore, some people in leadership positions come with a recipe for pain; do not mistake bad behavior for bad leadership. Lack of civility is not leadership.

> Leadership requires the ability and willingness to lead, and it
> is not based upon where you sit, but upon what you do.

Sure, good and bad leaders and leadership exist; examples of both can be found in world history and all the way down to our local communities. Even so, there is no need to continually qualify "leaders" and "leadership" with *good*, *great*, *best*, etc. With repetition, it gets to a point if "leader" or "leadership" is not prefaced with a favorable adjective (a qualifier), then we are left wondering if the absence of "good" means "not good." A slippery slope indeed. Besides, the dividing line between good and bad leaders and leadership often centers on moral judgments and perspectives that is beyond the scope of this book.

Finally, to know what constitutes leadership, we need to go beyond mere quotes, definitions, and descriptors. Instead, we need to train ourselves to *study what we see and hear.* Rather than saying, "I like that" or "I don't like that," or anecdotally commenting on what a leader did or didn't do, or said or didn't say, we need to diagnose *what we see and hear*—to break it down so we can learn from our observations. We will begin our study, or diagnosis, of leadership with two types of leaders.

FORMAL AND INFORMAL LEADERS

Generally, when someone speaks of a "leader" or "leadership," discussions drift toward organizational structure—namely leadership positions such as supervisors, directors, and so on. Even so, just because a person occupies a leadership position (at work, home, and elsewhere), does that make them a leader? Of course not. It is hopeful that this is the case, but occupying a leadership position does not automatically make one a leader, despite what Don believed. As mentioned, the two, *leadership positions* and *leaders*, are not synonymous. One does not necessarily come with the other. For example, a supervisor may not possess the willingness and/or ability to lead, and a person recognized as a leader by their peers may not occupy a leadership position. A quick review of our own environments will bear this out.

> Title or position does not make one a leader; nor does
> the absence of title or position preclude one from being
> a leader. Leadership does not discriminate.

Let us look at two types of leaders: *formal* and *informal* leaders. Note that Figure 1.2 acknowledges the existence of leadership as a precondition to types of leaders. If a person is not a leader, then *formal* and *informal* do not apply.

- ➤ *Formal leaders* are assigned leadership positions commonly found on an organizational chart; comes from job titles, financial responsibilities, and formal lines of authority that make up an organizational structure.

- ➤ *Informal leaders* perform leadership roles without having the official job titles or lines of authority granted to formal leaders. They are often referred to as *authentic leaders*: earned by who they are (personal influence, expertise, and social skills), not by where they sit or the position they hold.

Figure 1.2: <u>Leaders, Leadership Positions, and Types of Leaders</u>

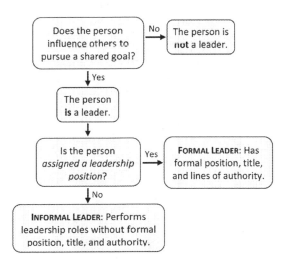

(Note: Figure 1.1 and Figure 1.2 are intended to illustrate leader/non-leader and formal/informal pathways. Leadership is not so linear; it is a complex process with varying contexts, environments, and feedback loops.)

It is common to have both *formal* and *informal* leaders present in the workplace. For example, when you need help with a technical matter, you turn to someone who has that specific expertise. That person could be the formal leader, but quite often it is an informal leader, a coworker or colleague. This should not be surprising; it is common for followers to have more expertise than their formal leader. Furthermore, an informal leader's expertise can have significant influence in the workplace. It is great if both *formal* and *informal* leaders get along, both on the same page and steering performance in a like direction. Unfortunately, *formal* and *informal* leaders do not always get along; conflicting views and contradictory instructions can pull followers in different directions and create stressful environments.

Here is an example: I have known Todd for five-plus years; he is Deputy Director for a large public utility. Though the deputy, he manages day-to-day operations of the utility (*e.g.*, chairs most meetings, leads most key decisions, coordinates with other departments and utilities, and briefs the Commission). Ben, the Director, telecommutes most days; he is in the office every Wednesday for a staff meeting and comes in a couple of times a week to meet with staff or attend a ceremony. Their relationship reminds me of the United Kingdom: the Prime Minister, Todd, *governs* the State, and the Queen, Ben, *represents* the State. I have seen it repeatedly, whenever something important comes up, people ask, "Where's Todd?" Ben is not even in the peripheral. I asked Todd about this curious arrangement. Though he does not have the title or position of Director, he does a bulk of that job and his too. "Yes," Todd said, "I love what I do, so I don't mind it." Todd may **not** be the utility's *formal* leader, by title or position, but everyone regards him as so.

Understanding the difference between formal and informal leaders, beyond position or authority, can be useful (see Figure 1.3). Even if someone is not officially designated a leader, it may turn out that they are considered to be one by the people they work with. Frankly, many employees take leadership roles and positions without having an official leadership title or formal authority. (Note: Not all descriptors of formal and informal leaders are exclusive; some descriptors may exist with both leader types.)

Figure 1.3: <u>Formal and Informal Leaders</u>

	FORMAL	INFORMAL
ARE	• Intelligent • Self-confident • Persevering • Greatly needful of power	• Intelligent, self-confident • Persevering, less needful of power • Likely to express sense of humor • Very well-spoken, self-aware
KNOW	• How to build a shared vision • More than his/her job's scope (familiar with others' involvement)	• Does his/her job well • The needs, values, and beliefs of others • How to build camaraderie and teamwork
DO	• Build relationships through diplomacy • Use formal authority • Communicate both formally and informally • Exercises authority conferred by position	• Deal with people informally; few formalities • Use stories to persuade/ encourage • Use inclusive approach to communication • Develop a vision based on shared needs, values, and beliefs

To reiterate, leadership does not discriminate; title or position does not make one a leader. We are hopeful that people in leadership positions are leaders, but one does not automatically come with the other. Likewise, the absence of title or position does not preclude one from being a leader.

Notice that discussions of leadership are not prefaced with workplace, office, corporate, or like terms. Formal and informal leaders exist at work, home, and elsewhere. The leadership role one performs at work—formal or informal—may be very different from the one at home, among friends, at church, and so on. Like the leadership quotes at the beginning of this chapter, the vast majority of them speak of a *leader* or *leadership*, not a formal position.

INFLUENCE: A FOUNDATIONAL LEADERSHIP COMPETENCY

Leadership is "the process of influencing the activities of an [individual] or organized group toward goal achievement" (Rauch & Behling, 1984). Whether it is formal or informal leadership, *influence seems to be a foundational competency.*

Granted, leadership is not solely founded on influence; one cannot influence anyone if credibility is in question. It is important here to mention the distinction between influence and manipulation. *Influence* is helping the other party achieve his or her outcome while you achieve your own. *Manipulation* is achieving your own outcome without regard for, or even at the expense of, the other party. Yes, you can make someone do something through manipulation, but that is not leadership.

When examining influence, it is often coupled with proximity. An example of *proximity influence* follows: I recently met with senior executives to discuss an issue that was challenging their leadership team. From the start of the meeting, two of the executives, seated side-by-side, fed off each other and dominated the discussion. Though others tried to contribute, they were shut out; efforts to achieve broader participation were unsuccessful. So, we took an early break, and I asked the dominating talkers if they would sit in different places when they returned—not sit together. They did, and within 10 minutes we were having a shared, balanced discussion. The proximity of the two executives sitting together was like a nuclear power source; they dominated the meeting. It took separating them to achieve full participation.

Another example of proximity influence that I am sure you have experienced involves highway driving. Often, I set cruise control when driving long distances. One of my driving pet peeves is when I am passing a slower vehicle and the vehicle I am passing—again, I am on cruise control—speeds up. Sometimes the vehicle paces me. What!? The presence of my vehicle influences the driver of the other vehicle to speed up. Similar behavior may occur on the way to a meeting: people routinely adjust their pace to be seen with a person of prominence in order to seek access or leverage, and commonly fall back or veer off to avoid contact with someone they wish to avoid.

I mentioned that our aim is to observe, diagnose, and study leadership, rather than simply seeing and anecdotally commenting on it. Instead of saying "I like that" or "I don't like that," challenge yourself to diagnose what about it you *liked* or *didn't like*, what specifically was said or not said, who was present or not present, and so on. Train yourself to observe, not just see, but *observe behavior*. When you do, you will notice some people are much more emboldened in the presence of a select circle of colleagues, yet quiet or reserved in the presence of others—proximity influence.

In addition to proximity influence, here are some other sources of influence[1] that leaders can use to *influence, even inspire, movement toward a common goal*:

- ➤ Perceived influence based on your TITLE OR POSITION. All supervisors, parents, etc., have some degree of this influence; the formal authority conferred to someone given their title or position.
- ➤ Others' belief that you could MAKE LIFE HARD FOR THEM in some way - ability to discourage unwanted behavior—compliance. If a follower performs a task poorly, they may receive an unfavorable performance review.
- ➤ WHAT YOU KNOW HOW TO DO - others' perception of the knowledge, skills, or expertise you have that could help them achieve what they need. Credibility and expertise on a subject carries weight and has influence on decisions.

---

[1] Other works relative to this discussion: *The Basis of Social Power*, French and Raven (1959), and *Management of Organizational Behavior*, Hersey and Blanchard (1982).

- ➢ <u>WHO YOU ARE AS A HUMAN BEING</u> - others' perception of who you are as a human being and how you make them feel (*e.g.*, valued or safe), which makes them like or admire you. People with this type of influence use their personal traits (*e.g.*, attractiveness) and/or interpersonal skills (*e.g.*, communication) to get their way.

- ➢ Others' belief that you could <u>GIVE THEM SOMETHING THEY WANT</u> - ability to reward desired behavior (*e.g.*, time off or increase in pay). Naturally, to provide incentives or fulfill someone's needs or desires, position influence may be somewhat a contributor.

- ➢ <u>WHAT YOU KNOW THAT OTHERS NEED TO KNOW</u> - others' perception of what you know that they believe they need. Can flow from position or personal influence. Who in the workplace has the most useable and reliable information?

- ➢ <u>WHO YOU KNOW THAT OTHERS WANT ACCESS TO OR TO BE CONNECTED TO</u> - others' belief that you know and have access to people who could benefit them. Also known as networking: it is whom you know.

Whether you are a formal or informal leader, all of these sources of influence are available to you; even an informal leader can have *title or position* influence, yet lack formal authority. At a minimum, you have the possibility of influence based on *who you are as a human being,* based on authenticity; you know, the kind of person with whom people want to be around. Successful leadership requires knowing when to use these sources of influence and in what combination. Good judgment and experience are required.

> Quite often, sustained influence requires a blended approach—rarely will just one source do the job. Moreover, what works well in one situation may not work well in another.

It is important to understand that influence is based on what we *perceive* (perception), not *what is* (reality); we cannot influence anyone to do anything. Yes, we can manipulate or force others into action through power or intimidation, but *influence comes from within*. To influence, we must create an environment within which others are influenced. For example, you may seek the advice of someone because you think they know what they are talking about—thus, you are influenced to seek their advice; but as soon as you realize their advice is flawed, what happens to influence? It dissipates, and it is unlikely you will seek their advice in the future. Again, we cannot influence anyone to do anything, but we can *create an environment within which others are influenced.*

In Figure 1.4, rate your sources of influence; indicate the extent to which you have each source of influence given a specific context (setting). It is important to establish context because the extent of influence you have at work may be very different from that at home or elsewhere.

Figure 1.4: <u>Sources of Influence</u>

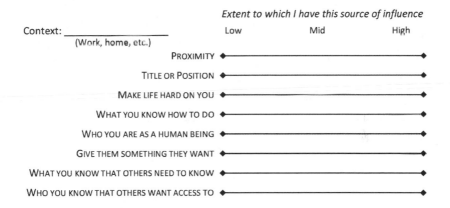

What are your main sources of influence? Are they where you think they should be? For example, if the only way you get things done is by making life HARD for coworkers, family members, friends, etc., it may be worth examining how you can increase other sources of influence. If you want deeper insight into your sources of influence, have someone in that setting rate you to provide feedback. What do you suppose the results will be? Mostly alike or different?

Pause for a moment and think of an example, good or bad, that influenced you (in your family, at work, in the community, among friends, etc.). Who is/was this person? How does/did this person influence you? What does/

did this person say/do? Who was present/not present? *Learn to observe leadership, diagnose it, and study it.* It is easier to do than you may think. For example, during your next business meeting, document on the margin of your meeting notes or agenda specifics about a leader's behavior and communication that you think were *appropriate* (+) and *not appropriate* (-) given the context. Use key words or symbols to record your observations. If useful, diagram table seating to document what you see.

My observations during a coaching session of an executive's business meeting are to the right. The purpose of the meeting was to elicit input from office managers regarding a service issue. The symbol "O" represents an open mouth; so, the annotation "O 12^+m" in the *not appropriate* (-) column means the executive talked for 12+ minutes before requesting input. The eye symbol "⊙" denotes eye contact. In this meeting, the majority of eye contact was directed at R (Roger); the executive failed to draw others into the discussion. Moreover, the table diagram shows the discussion was mostly between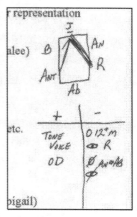
the executive, "J" at the top of the table, and Roger—lines represent number of communication exchanges. The executive never spoke to An (Annalee) or Ab (Abigail), or vice versa, which is why the mouth "Ø" and eye "Ø" symbols are slashed with "An" and "Ab" initials next to them in the *not appropriate* (-) column. In the *appropriate* (+) column are "Voice" and "Tone"; both were positive. "OD" are initials for Open-Direct dialogue, a real positive; but it would have been better if it included everyone.

As you can see, it is quite easy to document communication routines and behaviors that can be developed later into fuller leadership narrative. Try it. After doing this a couple of times, you will develop some of your own shorthand and find yourself diagramming exchanges in your head. Diagnosing what you see and hear will become second nature.

> Train yourself to absorb what you see—soak it in and then
> apply what you learn. The results will surprise you.

You can even ask a colleague to diagram and note communication routines and behaviors at your next meeting—one that you lead. Feedback regarding their observations can be very useful for improving group dynamics and performance.

REPUTATION IN LEADERSHIP

Building on influence, let us introduce reputation. *Influence* is your ability to sway others; it is an essential leadership capability. So much so, that John Maxwell said, "Leadership is influence—nothing more, nothing less." *Reputation*, on the other hand, is what you are known for: your behaviors, qualities, and skills as compared to accepted standards. Your ability to *influence* others is partly determined by your reputation; both influence and a credible *reputation* are leadership imperatives. You know the saying, "Your reputation precedes you." In other words, people hear and form judgments about you before they meet you. Consider the following biography:

> Originally, from New York, she is the oldest of four children. Working as a model, actress, musician, and book writer, she reportedly earned $7 million in 2005-2006. In 2005, she released a *New York Times* bestselling book. After losing her grandmother to cancer, she began regularly helping raise funds and awareness for causes, such as the fight against breast cancer and multiple sclerosis.

Does the narrative influence (or persuade) you to want to learn more about the person? Any idea who the person is? It is Paris Hilton. So, what does reputation do to influence? 👍 or 👎 Let us try it again. Here is another biography:

> Born to a Jewish family, he had early speech difficulties. Rejecting authority, he resented school and did not complete high school. Later on, he failed the entrance exam to the university. He was finally able to get a degree (mainly to avoid military service), but after graduation he was unable to get a job for two years. Finally, his uncle helped him find a job at a federal office as an assistant examiner.

Any idea who this person is? Albert Einstein. How about now? 👍 or 👎 Is reputation important? Absolutely! *Reputation partly determines the extent of a leader's influence.* It can give you a competitive advantage. It can help you achieve desired results. It lets you be regarded as reliable, credible, and trustworthy to employees, coworkers, customers, organizations, family, and friends.

My favorite quote on reputation comes from Benjamin Franklin: "It takes many good deeds to build a good reputation, and only one bad one to lose it." Being a golfer, there was a time in my life that I, as well as many others, held Tiger Woods in the highest esteem. Really, you say. Well, that was before we knew of Tiger's promiscuous behavior. Before then, he was known as a courteous, consummate gentleman; a loyal, happily married man and good father who would make any parent proud. My esteem for Tiger Woods was *influenced* by what I saw and heard—his *reputation*—not by who he really was. Recall, reputation is what we are known for, not who we are. The two can agree, but *what we are known for* and *who we are* may be a distance apart.

> One thing about *influence* and *reputation* is that no matter what they currently are, they can change—for better or worse.

What if you have a reputation of being a gossip—not networking or relationship building, but gossiping in the truest sense of the word? People seek you out for the latest scoop. One day you overhear someone refer to you as a "gossip." What? Me? A gossip? The thought of it stuns you. You are surprised anyone would think of you as a gossip. Sure, you talk a lot about people... Perhaps things started slow, a word here and there about so-and-so, more the following week, until idle talk become routine, a habit. But, being thought of as a gossip truly surprises you. That was not the intent in the beginning, but it ended up being the result.

Hypothetically, if this were you, a gossip, what would you say or do to change that? Like any habit or communication routine, the old, less desired behavior must be replaced with a new, more desirable behavior. It does not just happen; you consciously have to make it happen. You know when you go into work tomorrow, you will be presented with an opportunity to gossip; it is guaranteed. So, plan ahead: when the moment presents itself, what specifically will you say, not say, do, or not do in order to change the behavior? If you do not prepare, when given the chance to gossip, you will fall into the *same old way* communication routines; you will not realize the repeated behavior until it is too late. How many times have you have wanted to pick up something on the way home from work only to realize it when you are in the driveway? Habits can be powerful drivers of behavior.

The same, too, applies to desired behaviors. For example, you observe and study a colleague who has a great reputation, and you conclude that one reason for this is that she is really good at asking clear and cogent questions that reframe situations and drive dialogue. So, you work to authentically develop in yourself the same skill sets. This activity is **not** mimicking others to gain the reputation of a leader, but developing leadership abilities and behaviors as a result of persistent observation, study, and practice. Mahatma Gandhi said, "You must be the change you want to see..." If you want to be known as a *go-getter*, then be a *go-getter*. If you want to be known as being *timely*, then be *timely*. If you want to be known as being a *good listener*... You get the idea. Though there is no guarantee others will see you as a leader, it is important to be authentically you (and trust for the best).

In our hypothetical, if you do not want to be known as a gossip, then change the behaviors that lead to gossiping. It sounds simple, but habits can be hard to break. It is important to remember that *authenticity* is vital to creating and maintaining a credible reputation; should authenticity come into question, as in the case of Tiger Woods, then so too does reputation.

Suppose a boss, friend, or colleague brings your name up in a conversation, and then someone says, "What is he/she like?" What do you think they would say? What words (*e.g.*, polite, respectful, or honest) do you think they would they use to describe you? For example, would they say, "Oh, he is an overachiever who would cut your throat if you got in his way," or "She is really creative and a great team leader," or "He is polite and respectful and always seems to be there when you need him," or "She's not a team player." What are you known for? Think about it: if people were to describe you, not physically (*e.g.*, height, age, or hair color), but in characteristics (*e.g.*, trustworthy, good listener, or considerate), what words would they use? If you were to design your reputation, *what would you want to be known for*? Write a descriptor of your reputation goal in Figure 1.5. Perhaps one of the following:

➤ Sense of humor	➤ Trustworthy	➤ Good decision maker
➤ Honest	➤ Good communicator	➤ Good listener
➤ Professional	➤ Open-minded	➤ Considerate
➤ Respectful	➤ Inspirational	➤ Understanding
➤ Confident	➤ Impartial	➤ Approachable

Figure 1.5: <u>Design Your Reputation</u>

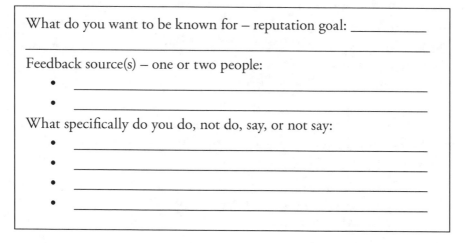

What do you want to be known for – reputation goal: _____
_____

Feedback source(s) – one or two people:
- _____
- _____

What specifically do you do, not do, say, or not say:
- _____
- _____
- _____
- _____

Relative to your reputation goal, who would you talk to that would honestly (with care and compassion) give you their feedback regarding your reputation? Put the name of the person(s) in Figure 1.5 - *feedback source(s)*. Requesting someone's feedback takes acceptance and courage; it goes like this: "I would like feedback on [be specific]. Here is why… [Listen] So, you are saying… Is there anything else I should know? Thanks for your feedback." While receiving feedback, try not to interrupt or be defensive. It is okay to ask questions for clarification and understanding, but do not cut the person's throat for giving you the feedback you asked for. It is important too that the person providing you feedback understands their role; it goes far beyond an initial session. Theirs is an ongoing role of continued feedback for a given period. For example, let us take the gossip hypothetical. Suppose one day the person who gave you feedback sees you gossiping. It is the feedback person's job to nudge you gently in the hallway, to leave a note on your monitor, or to do something that will help you refocus your attention on the new, desired behavior. Finally, given the reputation goal, write *specific behaviors, actions, and words* of what to do, not do, say, or not say in the space provided in Figure 1.5. Practice it until the new behavior becomes the reputation you want to be known for.

As you train yourself to observe, diagnose, and study what you see, you will discover that some of what needs to be improved resides with the person in the mirror. It is not "if I could fix everyone else, my problems would be solved." No, we have issues too. If you think not, just ask someone who has frequent contact with you. Knowing your reputation, and building and maintaining a good reputation is an important part of leadership. As you allow yourself to open up, you will find that there will always be things you can do to improve on who you want to be.

DEVELOPING LEADERSHIP BEHAVIORS

"The most important part of being a leader is maintaining the desire to keep on learning. That means learning about yourself, about your peers, and about the people you serve" (Brian Koval). When we open our eyes and minds to learning about the leadership behaviors of ourselves as well as others, we will find there are far more things that need attention then we have time to address.

Suppose the stick figure in Figure 1.6 is you. Next to you is a list of things that you have determined need improvement—derived from observation, self-assessment, feedback, etc. Since items on this list may pertain to others as well as you, which item(s) do you work on first? How do you choose? To prioritize the list, it is helpful to group improvement ideas—*things to work on*, based on your ability to influence its outcome (see Figure 1.6). Who is the one person over whose behavior you have the most influence? *You*. So, once items are in like groups, work on items that you have the most *influence* over first.

Figure 1.6: <u>Influencing Diagram</u>

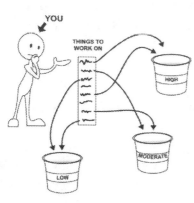

HIGH INFLUENCE: You have the influence, commitment, competence, and confidence to achieve a desired outcome.

MODERATE INFLUENCE: Need others' cooperation, support, or help to achieve a desired outcome.

LOW INFLUENCE: Can only encourage the outcome; have little to no influence on the outcome.

The reason to *begin with items that you have the most influence over first* is that you have only yourself to blame for getting in your way; you do not need anyone's permission to address many of the items in this group. If you started working on something from the *Moderate* or *Low Influence* group, you may quickly become discouraged and quit all together. Once you gain some success and confidence in improving those things you have *High Influence* over, you can move onto the more challenging items in the *Moderate Influence* bucket, and so on. Keep in mind that leadership is about *influence*; it is hard to control anyone, yet you can influence most everyone.

For example, an executive in one of my leadership sessions said the person who influenced him most was his father. As we all prepared a tissue for a heart-warming story of love and devotion, we were shocked by what unfolded. His father, he said, was verbally abusive to his mother and to him. Being yelled at and belittled by his father was a common occurrence. As a child, the executive had *Little to No Influence* over his father's behavior; but in adulthood, he had *High Influence* over his behavior. As a result, he swore that when he got married—which he was, and had a child—that he was going to be the best husband and father he could be. Influence can be both positive and negative.

As we have seen already, becoming a leader takes patience, good practice, and discipline. Leadership skills can be learned and developed, and quite often, results in behavioral change. As we all know, changing behaviors and habits can be difficult (*e.g.*, dieting, quitting smoking, being timely, or starting an exercise program). Stay focused and be patient; improvement will occur.

CHAPTER 2

LEADERSHIP STYLES AND PERFORMANCE

Every expert on leadership agrees that there is no one-style-fits-all approach to leadership. Jack Welch made this point clear: "[L]eadership is not just about you. It is about them." Put another way, leaders must tailor their styles to unite the unique needs of diverse people and changing environments. Leaders must be good readers of people and environments—not just meeting their needs, but adapting their styles to lead the way.

Too often, I see and hear people in leadership positions—notice I did not say leaders—speak of their "leadership style"—singular. The person's expectation is for staff to bend their will to his/her needs: "It's my way or the highway." In one instance, I heard a new director describe himself to his staff as a *hot head*. "I've always been a hot head," he said. "That's just the way I am, and you'll have to learn to work with it." Wow! What was amazing to me is that the new director spoke of his temper as though it was a badge of honor. Scary too, was his "getting to know you" speech was all about him—his wants, and his style—*me-me-me;* it was not about them, understanding their needs, or his vision for moving the organization forward.

Let me share a story about a one-style-fits-all approach to leadership. A manufacturing company having difficulties asked for my help. I met with the Chief Production Officer, who walked me through the plant and explained to me their biggest issues. Along the way, she introduced me to key staff that would be working with me on the project. On my return visit, I was asked to meet with the *new* Chief Production Officer. To my surprise, the person I met with last trip was gone, fired. The new boss sat me down, told me he was an expert in production, a proven leader, and that the company sends him to troubled facilities to "whip them into shape." Before I left—my consulting too was being dismissed—he shared with me his best practice for turning facilities around.

On the production floor, more than 100 production teams worked three shifts. The manager said that every Monday morning, first thing, he would bring the lowest performing team from the previous week into his office, berate them for their performance, and then send them back to work. Almost without fail, he said, the team would do better; this, to him, was a testament of his leadership. A testament, yes, but not of leadership.

His practice reminds me of probabilities and the bell-shaped curve. If you flipped a coin, what is the chance of getting heads? 50-50. If the lowest performing team was in the bottom 2% of production, what is the probability of that team doing better the following week? A 98% chance. Instead of berating the team, the new boss could have given them all a hug and performance would still likely improve over the previous 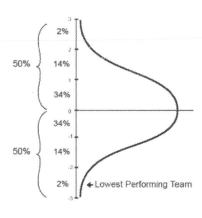 week. What the new Chief Production Officer was describing was variation and probability, not leadership. The only thing his actions did was drive talent out the door. Sadder still is the company rewarded the behavior.

One evening I watched a dog whisperer on TV. The subject of the show was a dog who had a very annoying problem of barking at everyone who walked in front of the house. The dog would begin barking as soon as it saw someone on the sidewalk, would escalate the barking as they neared the front of the house, and would not stop barking until they were out of sight. To the dog, the whisperer said, the passersby were intruders, so the dog barked to warn them away. Most passersby ignored the dog, but to the dog, them walking away was reinforcement of the behavior: its barking drove intruders away. This is worth restating: to passersby, the barking dog was nothing more than an annoyance; to the dog, barking was everything. Now, back to the *new* Chief Production Officer; he *was nothing more than a barking dog*. His behavior had nothing to do with leadership or improving performance, he was an annoyance; yet to him, his Monday morning ritual meant everything. Bad dog!

In this chapter, we will examine leadership styles, adapting your leadership style to meet diverse needs and environments, and the components of personal and organizational performance. Leadership styles and components of performance are coupled because both are normally needed to achieve desired results: leadership styles primarily focus on group and individual performance (people) while the components of performance focus holistically on organizational performance (people and other things). U.S. Navy Admiral Grace Hopper put it this way: "You cannot manage [people] into battle. You manage things; you lead people."

LEADERSHIP STYLES

If we believe as suggested by Daniel Goleman that "the best leaders... have the flexibility to switch between styles as the circumstances dictate," then the existence of each style must satisfy some particular need. If that premise is so—and there is broad agreement[2] that it is—then each *style of leadership* exists to address specific *group/individual needs*; and it is the presence of group and/or individual needs that prompt a leader's response (see Figure 2.1).

---

[2] Multiple sources: "Primal Leadership: Unleashing the Power of Emotional Intelligence" by Daniel Goleman, Richard Boyatzis and Annie McKee (2013); and "Management of Organizational Behavior: Leading Human Resources" by Paul Hersey, Kenneth H. Blanchard, and Dewey E. Johnson (2012).

Figure 2.1: <u>Group/Individual Needs and Leader Response by Leadership Style</u>

	GROUP/INDIVIDUAL NEEDS	LEADER RESPONSE
COACH/ MENTOR (C)	knowledge, skills, abilities, and confidence; motivation	develops competency and confidence; motivates
VISIONARY/ DREAMER (V)	clarity, sense of purpose and direction	provide purpose, focus, and clear vision
COMMANDING/ DECISIVE (D)	person in charge, situation control, decisive response	structure, instructions, decisive direction
LISTENER/ COLLABORATOR (L)	express their views, participate in decision making, get buy-in	listening, inclusion, collaboration
PEOPLE-FOCUSED/ UNIFYING (P)	structure, relieve stress, low conflict	harmony, mutual goals, team cohesion
WORK-FOCUSED/ PRODUCTION (W)	consistency, encouragement, accountability	high standards, challenging goals, performance monitoring

Let us check the premise: suppose a person has a fractured view of the organization and lacks clarity or a sense of purpose in what they do. As a result, the disconnect between *what they do* and the *purpose it serves* is detracting from workplace performance and personal satisfaction; it has created an "I just work here" mentality. So, given the individual's needs, what leadership style—leader response—would be most appropriate? VISIONARY/DREAMER: the leader needs to provide focus and a clear vision that demonstrates how their work fits into the broader mission. Likewise, if a group lacks the knowledge, skills, abilities, and confidence to do the job, then what leadership style, or leader response, would be most appropriate? COACH/MENTOR: the leader needs to develop group competencies and confidence by providing one-on-one time, concrete examples, and training and development opportunities.

Regardless of personal learning styles (*e.g.*, introvert or extravert) or personality type, leaders must be able to authentically convey—in words, voice, and body language—each leadership style when circumstances dictate. A discussion of each leadership style follows:

> COACH/MENTOR (**C**): Focuses on nurturing, developing, and motivating others; builds knowledge, skills, abilities, and the confidence to not only do a job, but to do it well. The 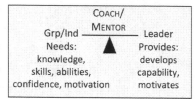 coach/mentor style of leadership is intended for those who *want to do the job*, but *do not know how* or *lack the confidence* to do it well. A coach communicates effectively; provides training and development opportunities, and challenging assignments to develop both capability and confidence; and provides one-on-one coaching/mentoring, concrete examples, a safe environment to learn from mistakes, and timely feedback to improve personal and organizational performance. The coach/mentor style encourages and motivates others and creates opportunities for people to lead when they do not have the title or authority to do so, thus developing the next generation of leaders.

Common mistakes of this style are micromanaging and putting people in a job, role, or position without developing the personal or professional competencies for them to be successful. Both mistakes are costly: *coaching people when they do not need it* (micromanaging), and ***not*** *coaching people when they do need it* (leadership neglect). Though micromanaging is an annoyance to those who have to suffer through it, neglecting those who desperately want and need help is a greater shame.

> VISIONARY/DREAMER (**V**): Visionary leaders provide a sense of purpose and focus. There are many examples of visionary leaders; we see and hear them in person and in media (past and present). These are people who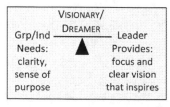

can *see clarity in chaos* as well as *articulate the way forward*; and as a result, people are drawn to them and their vision like moths to a light. Visionary/dreamer leaders must possess both abilities—*having the vision* and *articulating the way*—to be successful. I am guessing we can all recall a time when we have been in a position where we *knew the way, but lacked the words* to influence others to join us. It can be quite frustrating; if only we could get what is in our head to make sense coming out of our mouth.

The reason visionary/dreamer leaders are so successful in *having a vision* and *articulating the way* is in large part due to what goes in. The quality of what comes out (the vision and expression of the vision) is only as good as what goes in (awareness of surroundings). Visionary leaders get their input by being empathetic, patient listeners, and being aware of and attentive to both organizational and human contexts—values, attitudes, beliefs, and norms. These are learned abilities. It is the visionary leaders' understanding of these contexts that enables them to create and express their vision in terms and a manner that wins support. By being connected, they can express their vision in a way that inspires and rallies others to contribute to the dream; it influences others to translate vision to action.

➤ COMMANDING/DECISIVE (**D**): Provides structure, rigid controls, and issues instructions without asking for input. This leader exudes confidence, may have an intimidating demeanor, and

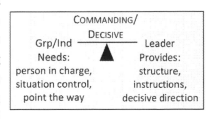

is not a good listener. I am sure you can imagine that this style runs the risk of contaminating others' mood, eroding motivation and commitment, lowering productivity, and driving away talent.

The commanding/decisive leadership style is appropriate in an emergency by providing decisive direction. In a crisis, people need

27

a decisive leader. It is a traditional military and strict hierarchical chain-of-command style and has a strong sense of urgency about getting things done.

> LISTENER/COLLABORATOR (**L**): A superb listener, collaborator, and influencer; persists in seeking understanding despite difficulties; and responds to comments (good and bad) in a way that reflects understanding. The listener values peoples' input—open-door policy. Unfortunately, this style runs the risk of appearing indecisive as when meeting drag on for days and weeks without progress. At times, what people need from a leader is a decision—enough talk, just point the way.

> > LISTENER/
> > COLLABORATOR
> >
> > Grp/Ind ———————— Leader
> > Needs: ▲   Provides:
> > voice their   listening,
> > views, buy-in   inclusion,
> > participation   collaboration

This style is very effective at building inclusion and collaboration. Experienced leaders realize that even if you know the answer, it may be unsupported if decided alone; sometimes it is wise to ask for input in order to gain buy-in. The listener ensures followers' voices are heard and valued in the decision-making process.

> PEOPLE-FOCUSED/UNIFYING (**P**): Promotes harmony, unity, and builds constructive relationships; relieves stress, recognizes the emotional needs of others, behaves professionally and supportively

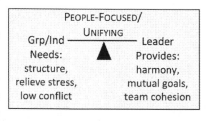

to create mutual goals, minimizes conflict and misunderstandings, and creates a warm, people-focused environment. This style of leadership is not all *kumbaya*, come and help those in need, or *group hugs*; it involves the hard work of building and maintaining healthy relationships and supportive work environments. People-focused/unifying leaders recognize and honor the emotional needs of the moment, and then quickly refocus attentions and energies on accomplishing the mission of the organization, family, or elsewhere. If not managed well, this style runs the risk of over-focusing on the emotional climate at the expense of day-to-day work.

The people-focused/unifying leadership style is crucial to leadership success. Unfortunately, some leaders mistakenly believe that a display of emotion or compassion is a sign of weakness; as a result, they seem cold, uncaring, and disconnected from the realities of life. Even our bravest and toughest military leaders give pause and reflection during emotionally challenging times. People-focused leaders know their people, their names, and something about each one.

➤ Work-Focused/Production (**W**): Has high standards and a strong drive for achievement; is performance driven, consistently maintains high levels of production, and painstakingly

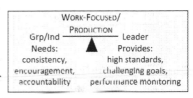

monitors performance. Works with vigor, effectiveness, and determination over a sustained period. Tends to create pressure, micromanage, and be numbers-driven. Work-focused leaders are low on empathy, collaboration, and patience, and run the risk of creating unrelenting pressure.

The work-focused/production leader is not a mean person; they are not rude, nor insensitive. All they want a person to do is their job; overachieving is fine, but failing to achieve to standards is unacceptable. *Do your job.* Look at how some environments operate: if you are a superstar performer, how are you rewarded? With more work. What happens to below average performers? They are often given less work. The result? We end up *punishing the superstar performers* with more work and *rewarding the below average performers* with less work. The work-focused leader holds people accountable: *you have a job to do, do your job.*

ADAPTING YOUR LEADERSHIP STYLE

Though we have looked at individual styles of leadership, in reality, a single leadership style rarely meets group or individual needs. As a result, leaders must blend styles to meet changing environments and diverse needs (see Figure 2.2). So, given the environment and needs at the moment, it may be suitable to have a customized leadership style for the office, family, etc., as a whole, as well as individual styles to meet specific follower needs; one may need mostly coaching, another visionary, and yet another commanding. With language, who determines if a communication was meaningful or not, the *sender* or *receiver*? The receiver, of course. So, too, is true with leadership styles: "[It's] not…about you. It's about them" (Jack Welch).

Figure 2.2: <u>Blending Styles to Meet Specific Group/Individual Needs</u>

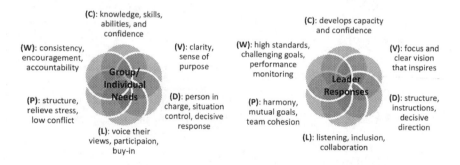

Effective readers of people and environments customize leadership styles to meet specific group and individual needs.

It is common for leaders to customize leadership styles—in words, voice, and body language—to meet diverse needs and changing environments. For example, if circumstances demanded a *people-focused* style and if in delivery you were in the person's face yelling, "SORRY FOR WHAT YOU'RE GOING THROUGH; LET ME KNOW HOW I CAN HELP." The person may have been better off if you said nothing at all. Yes, you may have spoken the right words, but delivery was out of place. In leadership, as for most all things, it is not just what you say but how you say it that matters. Leaders must master and authentically convey sequenced or blended leadership styles to meet specific group/individual needs.

Let us check our understanding of leadership styles using the following scenarios. It may be suitable to use a sequenced or blended approach. For example, start with mostly a *Work-Focused/Production* style followed by a *Coach/Mentor* style, or blending *Listener/Collaborator* and *Visionary/Dreamer* styles in order to address group/individual needs.

> ➤ Your new unit has suffered for five years under a terrible supervisor who screamed a lot at his employees. Morale is low.
>
> <u>What are *group/individual needs?*</u> Emotional healing, morale building, and confidence building
>
> <u>What *leader responses* are most appropriate?</u> Harmony and team cohesion (*People-Focused/Unifying*) followed by confidence building (*Coach/Mentor*)

> ➤ A unit is not performing well. The employees seem competent. The previous supervisor let them get away with poor performance.
>
> <u>What are *group/individual needs?*</u> Accountability (some tough love)
>
> <u>What *leader responses* are most appropriate?</u> Performance monitoring, and establish milestones and challenging goals (*Work-Focused/Production*)

> ➤ Your unit just got an assignment from the agency head with instructions to drop everything else. Your staff is competent but afraid they cannot meet the deadline.
>
> <u>What are *group/individual needs?*</u> Someone to take charge and confidence
>
> <u>What *leader responses* are most appropriate?</u> Decisive direction (point the way) and structure (*Commanding/Decisive*) followed by confidence building—provide one-on-one coaching and create safe environments for staff to gain self-assurance (*Coach/Mentor*)

31

It is understood that leadership styles must be administered within organizational constructs, so responses may vary. Even so, as long as we practice reading people and environments, a learned skill, our chances of getting the *right leadership style, sequenced or blended, for the situation* will be much improved. For those of you who enjoy fine Cajun cooking, you are probably familiar with the dark, rich roux that creates its roasted nutty flavor. To make good roux, you cannot rush the process; it must be developed at its own pace. The same is true for leadership: it takes practice and discipline to get it right—it, too, cannot be rushed.

Accompanying leadership is management; leaders must be good managers too.

> ➤ A *leader* creates a sense of purpose, develops and aligns people toward achieving that purpose, and motivates people to be successful.
> ➤ A *manager* plans budgets, staffing, and other resources; and provides and manages the system of service and production to support performance.

Even if a leader *leads well*, if they do **not** also *manage well*, performance will suffer. In other words, no matter how well you are staffed, no matter how competent, confident, and willing your staff may be, they cannot achieve desired results unless a capable system of service and production is in place to support performance. Leadership and management of the components of performance (see Figure 2.3) are needed to enhance achievement of personal and organizational outcomes.

Figure 2.3: <u>Leadership and Management</u>

THE COMPONENTS OF PERFORMANCE

People work in organizations, within and through processes and systems, to manage business and improve performance. So much of our lives are spent in processes and systems (*e.g.*, work, teams, and family), yet the composition or anatomy of performance can be a mystery. To manage and improve performance, we must understand the components of performance (see Figure 2.4). Wishes and hopes alone rarely achieve desired results.

Figure 2.4: <u>The Components of Performance</u>

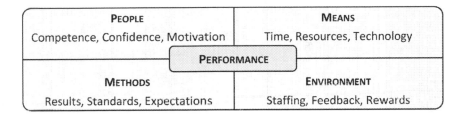

Leaders must understand the four components of performance: *People* (*e.g.*, competence, confidence, and motivation), *Means* (*e.g.*, equipment, materials, technology, and time), *Methods* (*e.g.*, processes, procedures, standards, and results), and *Environment* (*e.g.*, management system, organizational culture, staffing, feedback, and rewards). To achieve any undertaking (at work, home, or elsewhere), all four components must be present for successful performance to occur.

The four components enable leaders to examine and manage performance holistically, and it applies to any kind of performance (*e.g.*, individual performance, group performance, and organizational performance). The holistic view of performance is intended to broaden our understanding of what drives performance. Think about it: when something goes wrong, what often happens? We look for someone to blame—who did it (*People*)? This type of knee-jerk reaction occurs time and again; it is almost as if it is a conditioned response. Since other components of performance (*Means*, *Methods*, and *Environment*) are less apparent causes, they are often overlooked. As a result, when something bad happens, fault must belong to "who touched it last."

Consider this example: a person in a leadership seminar explained to me that in order to do her job (*Methods*), she has to print summary documentation to provide to clients for review and discussion. She starts her day early, usually around 6:00 am. Shortly into her day, the printer ran out of toner; unfortunately, the Office Supply Custodian does not get to work until 9:00 am. So, there she is (*People*); desperately wanting to do her job (*Methods*), but cannot because there is no working printer (*Means*). Not to be discouraged, she went on a search of other floors (*Environment*) to borrow a cartridge. Loss of workplace performance was **not** due to her actions; rather, it was due to *lack of Means*—no toner cartridge—and *lack of Methods*—no backup procedure to cover the absence of the Office Supply Custodian. Who is responsible for creating an environment to support performance? Management.

> No matter how competent and motivated a person is, if the *means*, *methods*, and *environment* are lacking, performance will suffer.

Each component of performance suggests possible questions to diagnose the cause of poor performance as well as possible corrective actions.

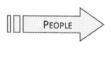

Wants to do the job but does not know how - **lack of competence**. Diagnosis Questions: Do individuals/staff have the knowledge, skills, and abilities to be successful? Do individuals/staff have the confidence to perform the job successfully? Corrective Actions: If no, arrange for formal training or coaching.

Knows how to do the job but does not want to - **lack of motivation**. Diagnosis Questions: Do individuals/staff have the commitment and motivation to be successful? Do individuals/staff support you and the work the organization is doing? Do individuals/staff share like priorities and direction? Corrective Actions: If the answer to any of these questions is no, consider the following corrective actions: talk to individuals/staff about how the job can meet their needs; surface disagreements; resolve competing priorities.

Diagnosis Questions: Do individuals/staff have the MEANS tools to get the job done (*e.g.*, technology)? Do the service and delivery systems and processes support performance? Do individuals/staff have enough time and other resources to do the job? CORRECTIVE ACTIONS: If no, change schedules, procedures, etc.; simplify the process; get new technology; give staff more time.

Diagnosis Questions: Do individuals/staff METHODS understand what needs to be done (results) and how well it needs to perform to be successful (standards)? Are expectations clearly understood, agreed upon, and achievable? CORRECTIVE ACTIONS: If no, accurately describe outcomes and verify expectations are understood, agreed upon, and achievable; identify clear, inspiring goals; agree on specific deadlines.

DIAGNOSIS QUESTIONS: Is the system of ENVIRONMENT management sufficient to support performance? Do individuals/staff get clear and consistent information (feedback) about how well they are meeting standards? Do individuals/staff believe they are doing well? Do you give like attention and support (rewards) to all performers? Are staff levels and staffing decisions consistent with workplace demands (present and projected)? Do staffing practices (numbers, skills, and experience) support performance—present and future? Are staff expectations changing? CORRECTIVE ACTIONS: If no or unknown, develop and empower process management; consistently give specific performance feedback; give poor performers guidance and resources—just as you do for high performers; create a supportive climate—be responsive to all staff; work within systems to attain the right levels and mix of talent to support effectiveness and competitive advantage.

All four components must be in place for effective performance to occur. Without competent and motivated *People*, performance suffers. Without the *Means* to do the job, performance suffers. Without the *Methods* to set expectations and describe desired results, performance suffers. Without a supportive *Environment* that enables people to succeed, performance suffers. The absence, in whole or in part, of any component of performance can adversely affect achievement of desired outcomes.

Review the following scenario: You have been the team leader for about two weeks. Marvin is a member of your team. Before your office began working in teams, Marvin was an average performer who met expectations. He did an average amount of work with generally positive results. In the last two weeks, Marvin's work has declined in terms of both quantity and quality. You have heard some of the other team members grumbling about Marvin not carrying his share of the team load. Marvin has a disability. → Using the components of performance as a framework, what may be possible reasons for Marvin's poor performance? For this scenario, I offer no interpretation of the narrative; responses to it are solely your own.

Now that we have an understanding of the components of performance, the next time something bad happens, pause to examine the whole system of performance instead of blaming "who touched it last." Effective leaders must understand changing environments and their impacts on operational work. In leadership, before you point, consider the problem may reside with you (Management - *Environment*), not the person doing the work (*People*).

Now that we have established the foundation of leadership and performance in Chapters 1 - 2, the next chapter introduces the critical leadership role of building and maintaining healthy relationships.

CHAPTER 3

BUILDING RELATIONSHIPS

In Chapter 1, we discussed the importance of influence in leadership. Consider this: *relationships are to influence what influence is to leadership.* In other words, it is the existence of relationships that creates the environment (whether intended or not) within which people are influenced, and it is the presence of influence that supports leadership. Sure, you can bully people, but that is not leadership. Here is a question for you: Does it take more than brains to be successful at work, home, or elsewhere? Of course, relationships—healthy relationships—are very important. Work happens through relationships; how people regard and act toward each other can greatly influence behavior, performance, and morale.

With whom should we build relationships? Supervisors, employees, peers, customers, stakeholders, family, friends, etc. Why is it important to build relationships? What skills do we need to build relationships? I have been asking people these questions for years. Specifically, I have asked them to write down *what comes to mind when they think of healthy relationships— word association.* Then I would ask them to tape their responses on the wall and walk around, reading what everyone has written. The discussions that ensue are amazing! Here is a sampling of responses:

➤ Respect	➤ Sharing/Listening	➤ Listening
➤ Good communication	➤ Trust/Trustworthy	➤ Understanding

➢ Honesty	➢ Selflessness	➢ Transparent
➢ Patient	➢ Nonjudgmental	➢ Supportive/Dependable
➢ Boundaries/Balance	➢ Open/Accepting	➢ Impartial

The above responses could go equally as well on your refrigerator door at home as they would at work. In this chapter, we will examine the stages of learning, leadership and emotional intelligence, and managing distressing behaviors (others' as well as our own).

WHAT WE DON'T KNOW CAN HURT US

Remember when we drew the stick figure in Figure 1.6? The stick figure was *you*; next to you was a list of things that need improvement. An important leadership (and life) skill is a persistent eagerness to learn about yourself—not just others, but you. A useful model that illustrates this ongoing process of learning is called the *Four Stages of Learning*[3] (see Figure 3.1).

Figure 3.1: <u>Four Stages of Learning</u>

UNCONSCIOUS INCOMPETENCE. You don't know *what you don't know or can't do.*

CONSCIOUS INCOMPETENCE. You are aware of *what you don't know or can't do*; so, you have a decision to make: do something to remedy it, or do nothing.

CONSCIOUS COMPETENCE. You can apply the new knowledge, skill, ability, or behavior if you consciously focus on it.

UNCONSCIOUS COMPETENCE. You apply the new knowledge, skill, ability, or behavior without even thinking about it.

Having taught in undergraduate and graduate studies for more than a decade, here is a college adaptation of this model:

➢ Freshmen **don't know** and *don't know they don't know*
➢ Sophomores **don't know** but *know they don't know*

---

[3] The model is attributed to Abraham Maslow.

> ➤ Juniors **know** *but don't know they know*
> ➤ Seniors **know** and *know they know*

The **unconscious incompetence** stage (or *ignorant bliss*) starts the process. This is a huge first step that many people do not even know exists. This stage is of great concern to national security, business, and individuals alike. It is at the unconscious incompetence stage where unknown *risks* and *consequences* reside—they are there, we just do not know they are there. Think about it: when trouble hits, accidents occur, or productivity plummets. We often say, "If only I knew, I would have…" For anyone who has young children or cares for them, you are constantly watching their every move: "Don't touch that" (it is hot), "Watch where you're running" (traffic), and so on. Children do not recognize the danger; it is there, but they just do not grasp the inherent *risks* and *consequences* of their actions. The reason so much effort is spent on unconscious incompetence is that *what we don't know can hurt us*!

In Chapter 1, we mentioned that you cannot manage or improve what you do not know. To manage or improve anything, you must know what you are managing or improving. So, there is the quandary: how do you know *what you do not know*? Truthfully, it is hard to discover on your own. It is like the discovery of the New World: the Americas were not new, they were always there; it just took Ericson and Columbus to point them out. So, how do we gain insight into behaviors—perhaps unhealthy leadership behaviors—that are there? Everyone knows of them, but to us they are transparent—obvious to others, but transparent to us. The answer is *feedback*—direct or indirect. (We discussed requesting feedback in REPUTATION IN LEADERSHIP.)

If you want to learn about yourself, then ask someone who knows you. Feedback can be a powerful gift of learning.

Then, one day, it hits you. Oh my, you realize—**conscious incompetence**, what others have known all along. It is like when you are at a social and someone points out that piece of broccoli in your teeth. You wonder how many people saw it but said nothing. You feel embarrassed. How could you get the broccoli out of your teeth if you do not know it is there? Why didn't someone say something? Yes, feedback can be a powerful gift; at least now, you can do something about it. I recall an attorney telling me that after doing the job for nearly a year, a senior colleague pointed out to him that he was applying a law incorrectly. Not knowing what you don't know can be a problem for you and others. Have you wondered why some people do not do their job? Perhaps, like the attorney, *they think they are already doing it.*

It is at the conscious incompetence stage (we *know what we don't know or can't do*) that we have a decision to make; namely, understanding the risks and consequences, do we minimize or eliminate them, or accept them, doing nothing? Recall the story of the new director who described himself as a *hot head*. Well, knowing you are a hot head is one thing; caring enough to do something about it is entirely different. Easy-to-anger tendencies can be managed; it starts with the willingness to do something about it. It is at the conscious incompetence stage when *risks and consequences* become *known*, that a decision must be made. Even if you choose not to decide, a decision has been made.

Suppose you want to do things differently—**conscious competence**—such as learn a new skill or behavior. To succeed, you must consciously focus on the new skill or behavior if you are going to apply it correctly; this new skill or behavior is **not** natural, or second nature, to you. Replacing an old behavior with a new one or learning a new skill requires conscious thought and conscious practice. Let us consider something as simple as learning to tie your shoes. It was not always so simple. There was a time when you did not know how, and someone had to do it for you. I recall when my grandson spent the weekend with us, and I wanted to teach him to tie his shoes. To me, the task was so natural that I could not think of the steps. When I tie my shoes, I do not think about it, I just do it. So, I had to take out a shoe and practice. That weekend, I made every excuse for us to go in and out of the house in order for my grandson to learn and practice tying his shoes. The new skill or behavior can be anything (*e.g.*, learning a new job skill, figuring out the coffee situation, learning the unwritten rules, becoming a better listener, or driving a car).

This stage is why the *Four Stages of Learning* is sometimes called the Four Stages of Coaching. To be successful, it is helpful to have someone, a coach or mentor as described in Chapter 2, to show you *how to do it* and *motivate you* along the way. The coach supports development by providing formal training, on the job training, mentoring, shadowing, rotational assignments, etc. So, when you are ready to learn a new skill, select your coach wisely; their role is to design and develop the materials and activities that you need to develop the new skill or behavior to the desired level of proficiency. Keep in mind that coaching works when there is willingness/motivation to learn and improve (*want to but can't*), rather than conduct/lack of motivation to perform (*can but don't want to*).

Finally, we reach **unconscious competence**; you apply the new knowledge, skill, ability, or behavior without even thinking about it. The new skill or behavior becomes second nature. Months after my grandson learned how to tie his shoes, a friend of his knocked on the door to play. In a flash, his shoes were on, tied (double-knotted), and he was out the door. Directive instruction was no longer needed, just support for a job well done. Once at this stage, regular self assessment and feedback is needed to ensure the new behavior or skill level is maintained at the desired level of proficiency. Otherwise, over time, you may find that skills and abilities decline or even revert to previous states.

Recall when you learned how to drive. Growing up you watched people do it all the time. It did not seem that difficult—you just get in and drive (unconscious incompetence). Then came a time when not knowing how to drive became a liability to getting around (conscious incompetence); so, you *decided* to learn the rules of the road and develop driving skills (conscious competence). Though an enthusiastic beginner, driving was not as easy as you thought, but in time you became proficient. Now, you just get in the car and drive away (unconscious competence); you do not have to consciously think about it: get in the driver's seat, put on the seat belt, adjust the mirrors, insert the key in the ignition...

LEADERSHIP AND EMOTIONAL INTELLIGENCE

Emotional intelligence (EI) prepares us for the slow and challenging process of building healthy relationships. Building relationships involves more than just doing the work—cognitive abilities; it is also about the people doing the work—emotions. Learning people's names and knowing what people want (*e.g.*, their goals and ambitions) from their work lives, home lives, and elsewhere are important leadership capabilities. EI seeks to balance cognitive (*e.g.*, rational thinking and technical expertise) and emotional (*e.g.*, thoughts and feelings) abilities to achieve effective dialogue and to build healthy relationships. Conversations build relationships, and healthy relationships happen one conversation at a time. Overemphasis or overreliance on cognitive abilities or emotions can have unwelcomed outcomes; balance of the two shows that there is more in common between people than just getting the work done. Exchanges that are rationally (cognitive) and emotionally (feelings) balanced create the interpersonal relations that are needed to manage the inevitable, hopefully temporary, conflicts and disagreements that occur when interactions turn from positive to negative.

> To build trusted relationships (*e.g.*, technical, social, business), leaders need to understand human emotions, recognize people's values, and be able to make connections with others.

Though there is agreement that IQ ceases to improve once the brain is fully developed, our general knowledge and emotional intelligence—the ability to know more—continues to improve. Goleman mentions that "emotional intelligence seems to be largely learned, and it continues to develop as we go through life and learn from our experiences—our competencies in it can keep growing."4 This is great news; similar to *sources of influence* and *reputation*, our level of *emotional intelligence* (EI), whatever it is, can improve. EI competencies (see Figure 3.2) that characterize outstanding leader behaviors are shown below:

---

4 A thorough discussion of emotional intelligence competencies is presented in: Goleman, D., (1998) "Working with Emotional Intelligence", New York, NY, England: Bantam Books, Inc.

Figure 3.2: <u>Leadership EI Competencies</u>

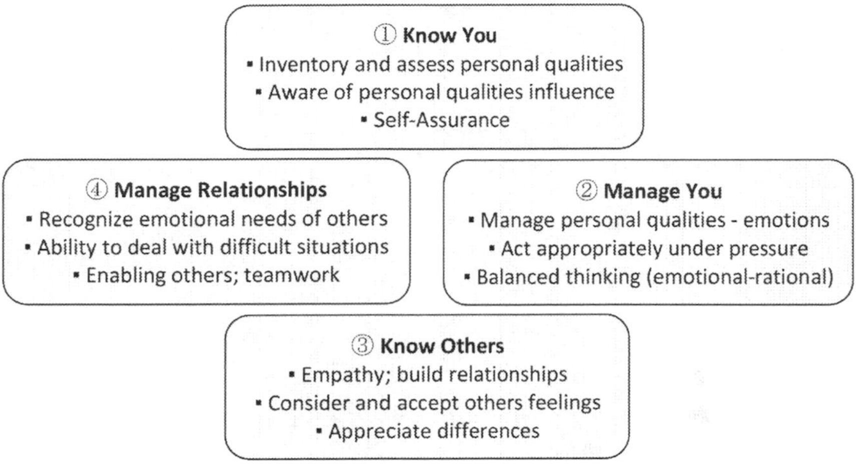

> ① **Know You**
> • Inventory and assess personal qualities
> • Aware of personal qualities influence
> • Self-Assurance

> ④ **Manage Relationships**
> • Recognize emotional needs of others
> • Ability to deal with difficult situations
> • Enabling others; teamwork

> ② **Manage You**
> • Manage personal qualities - emotions
> • Act appropriately under pressure
> • Balanced thinking (emotional-rational)

> ③ **Know Others**
> • Empathy; build relationships
> • Consider and accept others feelings
> • Appreciate differences

Explanations of each of these competencies follow.

You (Self)

①<u>Know You</u>: To have inventoried and assessed your personal qualities (*e.g.*, beliefs, attitudes, values, emotions, moods, and motivations), and to understand how these qualities influence your judgment, decision making, and behavior. In *Crucial Conversations*,[5] the authors write that knowing you "requires work. You can't simply drink a potion and walk away renewed. Instead, you'll need to take a long hard look at yourself." Joe Jaworski, formerly with Royal Dutch/Shell, reiterated this point: "Before you can lead others, before you can help others, you have to discover yourself."

Knowing you can be viewed from four perspectives (see Figure 3.3)[6]:

➢ *What you and others know about you*: Y, O
➢ *What others know about you, but you do not*: O, ¥
➢ *What neither you nor others know about you*: ¥, Θ
➢ *What you know about you, but others do not*: Y, Θ

---

[5] *"Crucial Conversations: Tools for Talking when Stakes are High"*; Patterson, Grenny, McMillan & Switzler; 2002 McGraw-Hill.
[6] Adapted from the Johari window.

Figure 3.3: <u>Perspectives of Knowing You</u>

You (Self) Continued

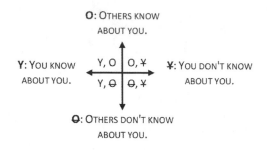

②<u>Manage You:</u> To recognize the effect that your personal qualities have on your ability to manage stress, act appropriately under pressure, and remain optimistic and persistent even under difficulty; and your ability to manage your emotions, express feelings clearly and directly, and balance feelings with reason, logic, and reality.

③<u>Know Others:</u> To build relationships through empathy and dialogue, understand the emotional makeup of others, consider others' feelings before you act, and have an appreciation of differences in how others think and feel about things—acceptance of others' opinions and perspectives.

Others (Social)

Likewise, *knowing others* can be viewed from four perspectives (see Figure 3.4)[6]:

➢ *What you and others know about them*: Y, O
➢ *What others know about themselves, but you do not*: O, ¥
➢ *What neither you nor others know about them*: ¥, ⊖
➢ *What you know about them, but others do not about themselves*: Y, ⊖

Figure 3.4: <u>Perspectives of Knowing Others</u>

O: OTHERS KNOW
ABOUT THEMSELVES.

Y: YOU KNOW ... Y, O | O, ¥ ... **¥**: YOU DON'T KNOW
ABOUT OTHERS. ... Y, ϴ | ϴ, ¥ ... ABOUT OTHERS.

ϴ: OTHERS DON'T KNOW
ABOUT THEMSELVES.

Others (Social) Continued

④<u>Manage Relationships</u>: To have an ability to manage emotions in a constructive way, recognize the emotional needs of others, able to maintain healthy relationships, and deal with difficult situations effectively.

Developing these four competences is **not** like, "Okay, got the first one done, check; now it is time to do the second one, check," and so on. No. Each competency is foundational and concurrent to the next. Competencies need to be developed in concert with one another; namely, get to *know you* first, then move to *manage you*, then getting to *know others*, and, finally, to *manage relationships*.

Managing these essential leadership competencies is like spinning plates. The object of plate spinning is to see how many plates can be kept spinning at the same time without one falling. It works like this: the plate spinner gets a plate (*know you*) spinning on top of a stick, then while the first plate is spinning, a second plate (*manage you*) is started on top of another stick. Though the plate spinner is focused on spinning the second plate, their peripheral vision is on the first plate. The second plate is not spun up at the expense of the first plate, but in concert with it.

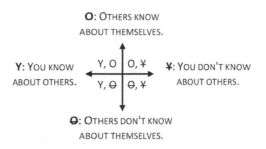

What would happen if the plate spinner took their eye off the first plate? It would lose rotation, begin to wobble, and crash to the ground. So, while you are learning to *manage you*, you have to be attentive to *know you*. Now, you have two competencies to keep spinning. In the sequence, it is important to *get you under control* first before you worry about others. Besides, I am sure we all have known someone who is an emotional wreck, where everything seems to be drama; they cannot even manage themselves, let alone manage a healthy relationship. The latter depends on the success of the former.

Once we have ourselves under reasonable control—an ongoing journey— we can move on to getting the third plate (*know others*) spinning. This competency requires us to take a personal interest in others (asking about their interests, concerns, family, etc.); it is the ability to read and understand emotional cues (empathy) and build relationships through dialogue. Managing three spinning plates may take some time, so do not rush it. When we are ready to move on, we get the fourth plate (*manage relationships*) spinning. The fourth plate involves collaboration, coaching, and inspirational leadership. Together, these leadership competences build and maintain outstanding leader behaviors and healthy relationships.

Let us check your understanding of these essential EI leadership competencies: Suppose you are walking in the hallway when your cubicle mate comes to you and begins complaining about a coworker. As he is telling you his grievance, he gets more and more upset, and he quickly starts cursing. What do you do? First, it would be helpful to get the employee out of the hallway; honor his emotion, yet get him to calm down as soon as possible. Then, focus attentions on your cubicle mate's beliefs and understanding of what happened—focus on behaviors, not people.

Test your emotional intelligence: what would you do in response to the following scenarios? More than one response *may* be appropriate.

Scenario #1: In one of your regular team meetings, John Doe cracks a racist joke. As the team lead, what would you do?
  A. After the meeting, quietly ask John to meet with you. In privacy, explain that making racist jokes is grounds for disciplinary action and warn John not to do it again.
  B. After the meeting, explain the incident to John's supervisor and suggest John be required to go to an EEO/Diversity training course.

C. Immediately stop John and say that these kinds of jokes are inappropriate and not allowed at your organization.

D. Say nothing because you are afraid that reacting to the joke will just call attention to it.

More than one response is most likely appropriate here; perhaps C followed by A. Given the behavior, immediate action is warranted. I know the adage "Punish in private; praise in public," but saying nothing may create the impression that you condone the behavior or find the joke harmless. Speaking up on the spot (professionally and respectfully) is appropriate. Sadly, B also happens; it is not just John who goes to training, but who else? Everyone present in the team meeting. B is only appropriate if John never attended EEO/Diversity training, or if he did not know such jokes were inappropriate and offensive. If John did know, then the issue is *conduct*, not training. D is likely inappropriate under most circumstances.

Scenario #2: In a staff meeting, Jane Doe, your colleague on the team, claims to have done the work on a project. The fact is that while this is a joint project with Jane, you actually did the lion's share of the work. What would you do?

A. Wait until the end of the meeting to speak with Jane. Tell her that in the future you would appreciate her giving you credit for your work.

B. After Jane finishes, thank her for her contributions and briefly add more specific information about your project.

C. Speak up on the spot and clarify that you did most of the work.

D. Keep quiet since you do not want to embarrass Jane in a public event.

Depending on the circumstances, all of the responses (individually or in combination) may be appropriate. What is not mentioned: Is this Jane's first offense, or her hundredth?

Emotional intelligence can help you think before you act, motivate others, promote better interactions, manage relationships better, generate willingness and loyalty, and deal with difficult situations. Getting it right is not easy, but if we fail to develop emotional intelligence in leadership we risk navigating difficult situations poorly, which in turn can have a powerful negative impact on our work and personal lives. Emotional intelligence is not about eliminating or controlling emotions; we are, after all, emotional beings. Emotional intelligence competencies exist to improve our leadership thinking and behavior.

HOT BUTTONS AND THE TALES WE TELL OURSELVES

Let us examine *knowing you* and *managing you* more deeply. We are emotional beings; emotions drive two responses: *feelings* (*e.g.*, happiness, anxiety, and fear) and *behaviors* (*e.g.*, laughing aloud, leaving an angry voice message, and cutting someone off in traffic). There is a part of the brain, called the amygdala, that is believed to initiate our *threat response*; it triggers a flight, fight, freeze reaction.[7] Whenever you perceive a threat, any threat (real or imagined, physical or emotional), the amygdala triggers the production of adrenaline that diverts blood flow *from* higher brain functions *to* your arms and legs for fleeing or fighting. As a result, people can be quick to act, moving from perceived threat to response in an instant. Rational thinking and thoughtful consideration, in that instant, are not priorities.

It is not just one shot of adrenaline that you have to worry about: Talking on their cell, a driver just cut dangerously close in front of you; you swerved to avoid getting hit. The *threat* of a near crash has your blood pumping; a *hot button* has been pushed! Angered, you raise your arms and shrug your shoulders at the driver. Then, immediately, the driver brakes in front of you and changes back two lanes; coffee spills all over the seat, another hot button has been pushed. Yes, situations can escalate. As soon as the second button gets pushed, you guessed it, another dose of adrenaline hits your system and the process reinforces itself. Now, you are double the emotion, double the trouble; unfortunately, it takes time for emotions to subside— they tend to linger around.

---

[7] More information on threat responses can be found in these sources: "Primal Leadership: Unleashing the Power of Emotional Intelligence" by Daniel Goleman, Richard Boyatzis and Annie McKee (2013); and "Crucial Conversations: Tools for Talking when Stakes are High"; Patterson, Grenny, McMillan & Switzler; 2002 McGraw-Hill.

Everyone responds differently to certain situations. Sometimes one person is irritated and upset by something, while others do not seem upset at all. This is because of our hot buttons: behaviors that aggravate or frustrate you, irritations and annoyances that provoke you, and feelings of being threatened, demoralized, anxious, angry, or frightened. *Each person has different hot buttons.* For example, some people may consider themselves to be a reasonable, rational person until they get behind the wheel of a car; then, it seem like situations outside their control transform them into another person. It is important to know what your hot buttons are so that you can manage yourself effectively; likewise, it is important to know others' hot buttons so you can manage conversations and relationships effectively.

Hot buttons trigger emotional responses and conflict in you and others. How many times have you said or did something during a confrontation only to regret it later? Likely, at least once. I am sure we all have left an angry voice message or sent a less-than-polite email or text message that, when clearer thinking returns, we wish we could undo. When we hear crazy, hard-to-believe stories of anger and rage, we wonder how rational people can do such things. Well, a rational person probably would not, but when emotions escalate, most anything can happen. *When emotions increase, rational thinking decreases* (see Figure 3.5).

Figure 3.5: <u>Brain Hemispheres - Rational & Emotional States</u>

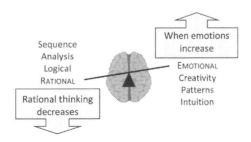

For example, whenever you are in a heated argument with a loved one, friend, or coworker, all you have to do is say to them, "Let's be rational for a minute," and everything is okay. That works, right? Of course not; that will likely make things worse, not better. *When people are emotional, they*

are not rational. If you and your friend were rational, you would not be arguing; fighting is an emotional response, not a rational one. Do not make things worse by continuing a futile conversation; tit-for-tat exchanges will only make things worse. Considerately disengage, then when heightened emotions subside and balanced thinking returns, think through your thoughts and intentions, prepare yourself and your listener, and focus on the cause of the difficulty, not the speech or behavior.

> We can either *manage our emotions* or have *our emotions manage us*—it is our choice.

Regardless of the intensity of the trigger or resulting response, *it is vital for rational and emotional states to be balanced* (see Figure 3.6). We need balanced emotional and rational thinking to effectively communicate, listen, and lead. Balance must be maintained (like the porridge story from "The Three Bears"): not too hot (anger and rage) and not too cool (lacking emotion and empathy), but just right. Emotional intelligence is critical for maintaining balanced mental states.

Figure 3.6: <u>Balanced States</u>

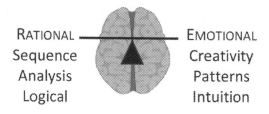

RATIONAL — EMOTIONAL
Sequence   Creativity
Analysis   Patterns
Logical   Intuition

> *It is vital for rational and emotional states to be balanced*:
> too little emotion can leave a person disconnected from the human experience, and too much emotion can cloud thinking and judgment.

Not all emotional reactions are intense; a gentle push on a hot button may result in a mild reaction. The extent of our reaction depends on the *hot button* being pushed (*perceived threat*) and who is pushing it. But in that split second between what we *see and hear* and *our emotional reaction*, a personal lens filters what we see and hear and what passes through to our consciousness is given meaning by our understanding of the context and our personal history, values, beliefs, experiences, etc. In other words, our response to what we see and hear is **not** based on *what actually happened*—the <u>facts</u>; rather, it is based on *our interpretation of what happened*—the <u>tale</u> we tell ourselves (see Figure 3.7).

Figure 3.7: <u>The Tale We Tell Ourselves</u>

Our response to what we see and hear is based on *our interpretation of what happened—a tale we tell ourselves—* not on what actually happened—the facts.

It is the tale we tell ourselves that evokes an emotional response. For example, your friend doesn't answer your text messages (*what we see and hear*), you think she does not want to hang out with you anymore (*our interpretation of what we see and hear*), and so you decide not to go to her party (*our response to our interpretation of what we see and hear*). Later she calls to tell you that she really missed you at the party, and that she is sorry for not calling sooner but someone stole her cell phone. Knowing what actually happened leads to an alternative tale with a different reaction, one based on *facts* and not the *tale* we told ourselves.

Recall the car you swerved to miss earlier. The tale we told ourselves was that it was just another rude driver who thinks they own the road, someone who deserved more than raised arms and shrugged shoulders. But when you saw the driver pull into a hospital emergency entrance, an alternative tale for the driver's behavior became possible: perhaps the driver was saving a life. *Tell yourself a different tale and you get a different response.*

> When we have a strong emotional reaction, we often
> look in the wrong place for resolution—*what happened*—
> rather than *our interpretation of what happened.*

One year, my son and daughter-in-law hosted our whole family for Christmas; it was great having our son, his wife, their three children, and our daughter (four months pregnant at the time) and her spouse under the same roof. The weather was great, and the company was even better. After the excitement of Christmas morning and before lunch, we decided to take a walk by the water. We were all ready to go except for our daughter and her spouse; the door to their room was closed. I asked my wife if they were coming on the walk; she didn't know. She said she hollered upstairs to their room, but there was no answer. Humm. What is going on? The closed door and lack of a response seemed impolite and rude—*the tale.* Are they not going to go on a walk with us? After about five or so minutes, I grew impatient; so, I sent my daughter a text message that read, "Unsociable?"—*the behavior* based on the *tale* that I told myself. I left with my son's family, and my wife stayed behind to bring my daughter and her spouse.

It was not until our drive home that I learned what happened, why our daughter and her spouse were in their room. While in the boys' room, one of the boys ran into our pregnant daughter's stomach. In some pain, she went into their room to lie down; her spouse went along to comfort her. Fortunately, the baby was well protected and all was okay. My reaction to my daughter being in the room was **not** based on what actually happened (*the facts*), but my interpretation of what happened (*the tale*). It was the tale that I told myself that led to my feelings (*e.g.,* disrespected and ignored) and behavior (*e.g.,* texting my daughter). Clearly, I misunderstood what I saw. Knowing what really happened, *the facts,* led to a different interpretation and response. I felt horrible; my daughter deserved better than that from me.

The *tales we tell ourselves* can consume our thoughts, sap our energy, and erode our confidence; so much so that they can distract us from work and life.[8] Our thoughts and the tales we tell ourselves can become unhealthy and self-defeating if left unchecked. For example:

JUMPING TO CONCLUSIONS: On the way into work, Bill gets a one-line text from his boss: "Call me ASAP." He thinks, "What did I do wrong?"

What happened: facts *(What we see and hear)*
Text message, "Call me ASAP"

The tale Bill tells himself *(Our interpretation of what happened)*
What did I do wrong? The boss is mad at me.

Bill's reaction: feelings and emotions *(Response to what we see and hear)*
Anxiety; Loss of productivity *Unable to focus*

As a result of the text message, rather than focusing on his work, Bill is in a panic, retracing his steps, trying to figure out what he did wrong. Granted, it would have been great if his boss provided him with more information, but it is Bill's interpretation of the text—his thoughts—that is causing him distress. To change his response, Bill needs to redirect his unhealthy, unproductive tales with more healthy ones, or at least acknowledge that without more information, it is just a text. Call the boss.

IT'S ALL MY FAULT: Anne is told by her son's teacher that he is not reading at grade level. Anne thinks, "If I was a better mother, my son wouldn't have this problem. I'm not good enough."

---

[8] More information regarding this topic can be found: *The Resilience Factor*, by Karen Reivich and Andrew Shatte, and from the work done on the topic by the Center for Continuing Education in Rehabilitation at Western Washington University.

What happened: facts *(What we see and hear)*
Anne's son is not reading at grade level.

The tale Anne tells herself *(Our interpretation of what happened)*
It's all my fault. I'm not good enough.

Anne's reaction: feelings and emotions *(Response to what we see and hear)*
Sadness, depression *Misses causes of the problem*

No matter what happens, Anne internalizes problems that happen around her as her fault; she thinks if only she was a better mother, person, leader, etc., she could prevent bad things from happening. Commonly heard from Anne are her apologies for *not catching the mistake*, for *not seeing that one coming*, for *not knowing that would happen*, for *not…* Anne needs to evaluate and redirect her thinking, and consider the circumstances that led to the undesirable outcome (*e.g.,* what others may have done or how other environments, other than her own, may have contributed to the situation).

IT'S NEVER MY FAULT: Alex is having difficulty completing projects on time. He thinks to himself, "It's not my fault; no one can succeed around here."

What happened: facts *(What we see and hear)*
Projects not completed on time

The tale Alex tells himself *(Our interpretation of what happened)*

Not my fault. Boss is being unreasonable.	

Alex's reaction: feelings and emotions *(Response to what we see and hear)*
Anger - not my problem *Does not address the problem*

Alex has the opposite mindset of Anne. Where Anne *internalizes* what happens, Alex *externalizes* most everything; it is never his fault.

FIXATING ON THE BAD: Jane is presenting her team's progress to a group of peers and a senior manager. Two peers have good eye contact, two are asking good questions, one answers her cell phone and leaves the room, two are exchanging comments, and the manager listens and nods but yawns at one point. Jane thinks, "This presentation is going poorly."

What happened: facts *(What we see and hear)*
Presentation (cell phone, yawn, etc.)

The tale Jane tells herself *(Our interpretation of what happened)*	
I'm a poor presenter. People think I'm unprepared, mismanaging.	

Jane's reaction: feelings and emotions *(Response to what we see and hear)*
Anxiety, sadness, depression *Performance declines*

Jane fixates on what she perceives as the bad things that happen; she ignores the good things. As a result, she fails to see the situation as a whole.

It is important to understand that *the tales we tell ourselves are not facts*; they are tales formed by our beliefs, education, backgrounds, biases, political affiliations, gender, ethnicity, etc. For example, if I gathered people in a room and asked each person to count the number of people in the room and then reveal their count, do you think they would get the same number or different numbers? The same, of course. Our beliefs, background, religious affiliation, sexual orientation, and so on have no bearing whatsoever on counting the number of people in the room; counting people is *objective*, a *fact*. But, if I asked the same group to count the number of people in the room that they think are *nice*, do you think they would come up with the same number or different numbers? Likely different numbers. Now, each person's background, history, experiences, and so on would determine who in the room is "nice." Who is nice and who is not is *subjective*; it is based, in part, on the *tales* we tell ourselves.

Suppose a year later I gather the same people to repeat the exercise. First, they count the number of people in the room and reveal their count, same number or different? Same. Now, the number of people in the room that they think are nice, same number or different? Different. Would the number of nice people be the same as last year's count? Unknown. Last year you thought so-and-so was nice, but not this year. Facts are undisputed—the passage of time does not alter their outcome; however, the tales we tell ourselves can change over time as our biases, experiences, education, etc., evolve. I am sure many of us can remember a time when our beliefs regarding something or someone changed. Maybe they seemed good at the time, but over time things (and our beliefs regarding them) can change.

When personal lenses and filters (*e.g.*, backgrounds, experiences, histories, biases, perceptions) go unchecked, they can lead to unhealthy beliefs, attitudes, and behaviors. As mentioned, you cannot manage what you do not know; so, stay tuned to you and connected to others. Leadership requires proficiency in all four EI leadership competencies. Knowing and managing your thoughts and intentions, as well as distinguishing tales from facts, are core leadership competencies.

MANAGING YOU: BEING RESILIENT

Let us go back to *hot buttons*, something that evokes an
emotional response. Whose *hot buttons* are they? Yours.
That is right; so, here is the truth about "hot buttons":
No one can push your buttons—they are your buttons, you
own them. Yes, you can give others the power over them,
but they are your buttons. We let them get pushed. This
reminds me of the quote: "Life is 10% what happens to you
and 90% how you react to it" (Charles R. Swindoll, 1934).

One way to remain cool under pressure is to *know your environment*—what
you are walking into—and to rationally think through (ahead of time)
your response to it. During the holidays, it is common to see articles that
help people cope with the emotional difficulties of family gatherings; no
one knows better than families how to push your buttons.

> ➤ *Know Your Environment*: You do not choose who you want to work
> with each day, nor do you choose the family you are born or marry
> into. You get what you get. So, when families come together for
> the holidays, it can be an *interesting gathering* (*e.g.,* so-and-so will
> not sit next to you-know-who, your wife and daughter-in-law are
> not speaking to each other, and so on).
>
> ➤ *Your Response to It*: You do not own the *environment* and likely
> have little to no influence over it; what you do own and have
> influence over is your *response to it.* Plan ahead. Think through the
> inevitable smirk or quip intended to get you riled up. *Don't give*
> *people power over your emotions and emotional reactions*!

During lunch at a client location, I was prepping for the afternoon session.
Someone unfamiliar to me walked into the boardroom and switched a
special ergonomic chair with an ordinary chair from another person's
place at the table. Observing this, I asked the person if I could be of any
help. "No," the person replied, "it is just Bill, and we all mess with him;
sometimes we put his chair in the hallway." Rather than moving the chairs
back, I waited to see how it would unfold.

Sure enough, noticing his chair was moved, Bill walked over to read the name of the person on the tent card. "Oh," he said, "she thinks she can take my chair." I quickly shared with Bill what had happened and with a huff, he shook his head. Bill just let his office mates push his button. I shared with Bill that *knowing his environment*, if he could keep his cool and *respond* differently, the pranksters in his office would find another outlet to occupy their attentions. Months later, Bill sought me out when I was back onsite. He said he took my advice and nowadays, no one moves his chair; work life is good and he's *cool*.

> No one can push your "hot buttons"—they are your buttons,
> you own them. You let them get pushed. *Don't give people
> power over your emotions and emotional reactions!*

Since you have been in the new office, each morning you have greeted your coworker with, "Good morning." Without fail, you get no response, not even recognition that you walked in the office. You know the *environment* you walk into each morning—that you have *little to no control over*. What you do have control over is your *reaction to it*. Are you going to give your coworker power over your behavior? You are not the kind of person who doesn't say, "Good morning." That would be uncivilized. So, you decide to keep being you, upbeat and civil. "Good morning, Sam."

A technique that I find helpful to transition someone, including myself, from a heightened emotional state to a balanced mental state is illustrated in Figure 3.8. It begins by **acknowledging** the person's issue/emotions; in other words, displaying empathy. Sometimes, a person who is emotionally upset just needs a moment to vent and wants others to acknowledge their issue/emotions. Some venting is okay, but move on as soon as you can. Acknowledgment lets the person know you have listened to and understand their issue/emotion—not that you agree with them, but that you have listened to them. Acknowledgement can be conveyed by saying something like, "It seems you are quite upset by the..." or "I know it can be frustrating to..." or "You must have been angry to learn..." or "I'm sorry that happened."

Figure 3.8: <u>Transitioning to a Balanced Mental State</u>

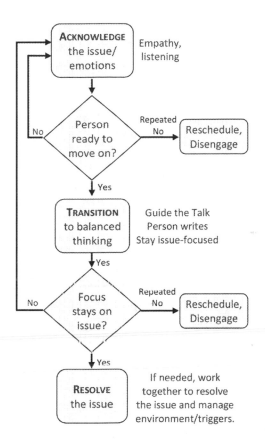

As soon as the *person is ready to move on*, **transition** the person—guide the talk—from expressing emotions to writing on a piece of paper their interpretation of what happened as well as their beliefs regarding why it happened—the person experiencing the heightened emotion does the writing. Think about it: in order to write, a person must think sequentially—sequence the letters to form words, sequence words to form sentences, and so on. The activity of writing becomes the calming agent that transitions thinking from a heightened emotional state to a balanced mental state; it creates a rational frame of mind that allows a person to reason instead of react. Moreover, the time it takes a person to compose and manually write their thoughts is often sufficient enough to allow the adrenaline to flush from their system and for clearer thinking to return.

Frequently, after several short paragraphs, writing is no longer necessary because it has served its purpose. Balanced thinking is restored.

Now, our job is to keep thinking balanced and to *focus* the person's attention on managing their environment/triggers and **resolving** the issue: "I felt [emotion] when…and interpreted it as…"

Knowing and managing *you*, keeping cool under pressure, responding appropriately, and connecting with others will go a long way toward building and maintaining healthy relationships at work, home, and elsewhere. Our relationships are critical to influence and leadership.

CHAPTER 4

THE ART OF COMMUNICATION

Effective communication is indispensable to leadership: conversations build relationships, relationships promote influence, and influence is vital to leadership.

Unfortunately, many people in leadership positions are overtasked and overburdened with way too many things to do; as a result, communication is often rushed, incomplete, or vague. Receivers, too, are very busy and often get caught trying to figure out a leader (or executive) wants. So, they throw something together and send it back to the leader hoping it will stick. Now it is the leader's turn: they have to read the receiver's reply and their original request, then reply back to the receiver with more specifics to get what they want, and so on. By the time effective communication happens, the information is too late; a decision has already been made. Not being clear about what we mean and not listening to what is said often gets in the way of effective leadership, relationships, and performance. In this chapter, we will examine aspects of communication, the communication process, communication styles, listening, and responding.

Sadly, effective communication is viewed by many people as a consumer of precious time, not a saving of it. In many instances, a few seconds more to complete a communication would get people what they want sooner and save everyone's time in the process. To illustrate, an executive sent a staffer the following email: "Send me what you have on the inquiry ASAP." The staffer thought: "Okay… Which inquiry?" Managing and responding to inquiries is the staffer's job; they do it all workday long. Which one of the nearly two dozen inquiries on the staffer's desk does the executive want information on? Beyond identifying the inquiry in question, what specific information is needed? Work and life are already hectic enough; most people are already overworked, and many workplaces are already understaffed without making matters worse. Communicating clearly saves time, not wastes it.

> Rushed, incomplete, and vague communication causes
> more work, not less; it consumes more time, not less.

Including work, much of today's communication is conveyed by text, voice, social media, etc. That is not surprising or unusual; entire conversations can consist of brief exchanges of emails or text messages. For example, if I called any contact (family or business), at any time of the day, it is unlikely my call would be answered. Yet, if I sent a text message, I would likely get a prompt reply. I am not knocking it. Texting is a very effective means of communication and serves a valuable purpose, but when you have something really important to say, when understanding and being understood is imperative, when it really matters, adding voice, or voice and body language, can greatly enhance communication.

Not long ago, I was coordinating an upcoming visit with a client across time zones. Since the client was rarely in their office, communicating via email and text message usually worked best. However, in this instance, the back-and-forth emails and text messages were taking way too long; we had been at it for two days already. I thought if we could just talk for a few minutes, we would get everything done. So, I texted if we could finish up on the phone. He replied, "k." Perfect, so I gave him a call. Immediately he texted me, "It's not a good time." Huh!? His reply baffled me. Later, my client called to apologize for not being able to talk earlier; he told me the office was in meltdown. "No problem," I said. "I thought '*k*' meant that it was okay to call." "No," he replied, "'*k*' meant it was okay for to us talk, but not then." Interesting how the same words, a letter in this case, can mean and be interpreted differently by different people.

If had we talked on the phone, I am certain that I could have sensed the stress and frustration in his voice (tone, pitch, inflection, speed, and volume) and understood it was not a good time to talk. Adding voice to words greatly enhances our ability to convey and interpret meaning. Language is powerful, yet complicated. Using our voice (vocal qualities), we can say the words yet mean the opposite. You try it: say, "Oh, yea, *you're right*," while using your voice to convey the opposite. We can also communicate that we are annoyed without using words at all, just body language. I recall a senior staff meeting when an executive briefed a new rule change that was going to affect the entire organization, a necessary change that was believed to better align businesses and improve performance. With a grimace, another executive replied, "*Great. Appreciate your help*." Though the words were spoken, gratitude was never conveyed.

Though we do it all the time—communicate—you would think we would be better at it. Unfortunately, mixed messages, vague communication, and unclear intentions are a common occurrence. We often hear people say, "Oh, sorry, I know that's what I said, but I meant..." or "No, no. That's not what I intended." Since we are all so very busy, having more things to do and say than we have time to do and say them in, we rush messages in hopes that the receiver can untangle and decode our fuzzy, cryptic words.

Let me set the context for this chapter: it is **not** about water cooler chitchat or casual conversations; though the lessons learned (or relearned) here will help with that too. This chapter focuses on those occasions when you need to do everything you can to get the message right—*sent as intended* and *received as desired*. When conversations really matter, we cannot leave them to chance.

ASPECTS OF COMMUNICATION

As a refresher, communication "is the activity of conveying information through the exchange of ideas, feelings, intentions, attitudes, expectations, perceptions or commands, as by speech, gestures, writings, behavior."[9] Each aspect of communication—*verbal, vocal qualities,* and *body language*—conveys meaning. In other words, meaning is derived by interpreting the words we use (*verbal*), how we say them (*vocal qualities*), and *body language* (see Figure 4.1). Effective communication aligns all three into one message, one meaning. The percentage that we rely on each aspect of communication to interpret the meaning of what was said follows.[10]

Figure 4.1: <u>Aspects of Communication</u>

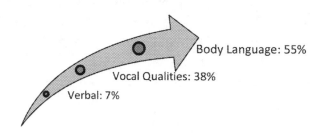

Body Language: 55%

Vocal Qualities: 38%

Verbal: 7%

Verbal (actual words) is not too surprising, only 7%. It is not the word that conveys meaning; rather, it is the context within which the word is used that conveys meaning. Look up any word in the dictionary; likely, it will have multiple meanings. You try it: what does "lead" mean? Not sure without the context of use. Is it "to go in front of," or is it "a metal"? Both words are spelled the same, but they sound different and have different meanings. Same is true for "live": *live* animals or *live* well? Without context of use, we are unsure how to read or pronounce many words. Similar too are words that sound the same but are spelled differently: two, to, and too; there, their, and they're. Even the common meaning of words vary: for many, a *tablet* is no longer something you take in the morning; it is a small, single-panel computer.

---

[9] Harper, Douglas. "communication". Online Etymology Dictionary. Retrieved 2013-06-23.

[10] Multiple sources: Albert Mehrabian, Ph.D., *Silent Messages* (1971) and *Nonverbal Communications* (1972); Barbara and Allan Pease, *The Definitive Book of Body Language* (2006); Sue McCarthy, *Body Language* (2013).

The words we choose to use and how we interpret them are commonly based on our age, gender, background, experience, education, etc. The words alone is what caused me to misunderstand the texted message *"k."* Since words lack the emotions that are conveyed in voice and body language, we have traditionally used **bold**, *italics*, <u>underscore</u>, and exclamation points to show emphasis. Today, text messages frequently use emoticons (☺) to convey or enhance meaning. The point is, words alone are rarely adequate to support crucial conversations; voice, or voice and body language, is often needed.

Vocal qualities (how we say words) are important, 38%. Like the executive's reply, *"Great. Appreciate your help,"* make certain that your tone is in sync with your words; otherwise, the words may not be interpreted as authentic. The tone of our voice can completely contradict the words. Sometimes, it is not *what you say* but *how you say it* that offends people. Tone is how we convey sarcasm; it can greatly influence how a message is interpreted. For example, a polite tone may convey openness while a monotone voice may indicate boredom. Emphasis (inflection) also makes a difference: I didn't *say* you were stupid. I didn't say *you* were stupid. I didn't say you were *stupid*.

Body language, 55%, is not an exact science, yet body language often conveys more of our message than words and vocal qualities. The signals body language send are often a reliable indicator of what we are really thinking and feeling. With body language—use of posture, facial expression, eye contact, use of personal distance, body movement, or gesture—we do not even have to say a word, yet we can speak volumes. Furious with his coworker's response, he turned and walked away. "What?" the coworker said, "I didn't say anything." "You didn't have to," he replied. "The look you gave me said everything."

Recently, I was working with an executive team on a project when the CEO dropped by to thank me for helping them with a difficult issue—all the while he was reading a message on his BlackBerry. For the length of the message, he never made eye contact with me. His body language drowned out his words. When what we hear does not match what we see, which do we believe? We all know that it is what we see.

Getting the three aspects of communication synchronized is crucial if we are to be authentic. Leading authentically requires that our words, voice, and body language be in agreement—aligned—so the receiver is focused on the message. What happens when you are reading an important document and come across a typo or misspelling? It distracts you; rather than being focused on the message, you become an editor on the hunt for the next error. The same too is true with communication. When our words, voice, and body language do not agree, the receiver is distracted by multiple messages. They are left wondering: What is the real message? Which one do I believe?

> Meaning is derived by interpreting the words we use, how we say them, and body language. Effective communication aligns all three into one message, one meaning.

Sam and Kelly were going out for a romantic dinner, one that both had been looking forward to for a long time. Before leaving the house, Sam posted on Facebook their big plans for the evening. To be honest, Kelly had been becoming increasingly frustrated with Sam's obsession with Facebook. While at the restaurant, he checked to see if anyone *liked* his post. While there, not to be disrespectful to his *friends,* he responded to and *liked* others' posts. The romantic evening between two lovers had become a threesome—Sam, Kelly, and Facebook. Kelly felt disrespected, even threatened, that Sam was more interested in his *electronic relationships* than the one sitting across the table. So, having her *hot button* pushed, she bellowed, "Put the…phone away!" Sam looked at her like she was crazy. "What? I was just checking Facebook," he said. "It's no big deal." → It is a very big deal. Now, dinner is reserved for just the two them. Facebook stays home with the dog.

THE COMMUNICATION PROCESS

As a refresher, let us examine the communication process (see Figure 4.2). Though our focus is on critical conversations, everything we will discuss applies to informal ones as well. When what we have to say matters so much that we need to do everything in our power to achieve the desired outcome, we need to study up—getting it wrong is not an option.

Figure 4.2: <u>Communication Process</u>

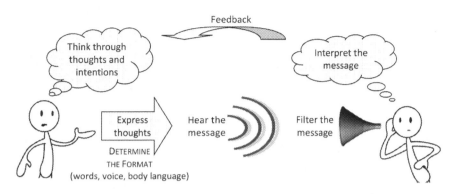

Again, in language, who determines whether a communication is meaningful or not, the sender or receiver? The receiver. So, when composing your **thoughts** and **intentions**, you need to do so with the receiver in mind—their background, culture, history, etc. How someone communicates with a client is likely very different than with a friend, coworker, boss, etc. Audience matters. The words you use or avoid using, and how you say them, depend on the audience (the receiver, who you are talking to). You have to think through the *intent of the communication*, the purpose. What do you want the receiver to take away from your message? How do you want them to feel after hearing your message? Know your audience.

Assuming you have done a good job gathering your thoughts and intentions, you need to determine the best *format*—face-to-face, phone, text message, etc.—to convey the message. Here, too, it is not what you say but how you say it (format) that counts. For example, Ben was a dedicated member of the staff who truly believed in the work and the people he served. Going above and beyond day after day was just something he did, and customers and staff greatly appreciated him for it. One day, Ben had a voice message from a senior executive thanking him for his service. What! A voice message? He thought if the executive truly appreciated his work, he would have walked down the hallway and told him in person. Their offices are on the same floor; it would have taken less than five minutes for the executive to convey a simple "Thank You" in person. Instead, Ben got a voice message; he was insulted that the executive did not care enough about his performance to get out of his seat and tell him in person. Format matters.

Several years ago before Christmas, my son called me with news that he got the big promotion and that he and his family would be moving to Manhattan. "Awesome," I said. "I am so excited for you and your family. What an experience to live and work in Manhattan." While we talked, I walked out to our patio so my wife would not overhear our conversation. When we finished talking, my son asked if he could talk to Mom; he wanted to tell her the good news. "No," I said, "that's not the kind of news you tell your mother over the phone. Instead, let's do this: all of you come to the house this weekend. I will take the children on a walk, and the two of you (son and daughter-in-law) can tell Mom the news face-to-face." Knowing the audience, my wife, I knew the news would devastate her. A text message or call would not work. Know your audience; format matters.

At this point in the communication process (composing your *thoughts* and *intentions*, and determining the *best format*), we have not spoken a word; it has all been planning the communication. Now, it is time to *express your thoughts*. Whatever we say will likely be filtered and interpreted by the receiver's assumptions, biases, preconceptions, stereotypes, past experience, etc. Filters can influence what we recognize (see and hear). There was a time when I owned a Prius. Before I bought one, I never knew what a Prius looked like, never recalled seeing one on the road. Once I owned one, I saw them everywhere. Where did they all come from? They were there all along; my perceptual filters had changed.

Filters have a powerful influence on communication; when what we see and hear is consistent with what we believe, they are accepted without much scrutiny. However, if what we see and hear challenges established beliefs, they can be dismissed without recognition or undergo intense scrutiny. Because beliefs, assumptions, biases, preconceptions, etc., have such an influence on communication, judgment, and decision making, it is important that we account for their presence. Others may not share our view of the world.

Recall from our discussion of hot buttons in Chapter 3: when emotions go up, rational thinking starts shutting down. So, as we compose our *thoughts and intentions*, we need to do so in a means and manner that **keeps the**

receiver focused on the message (whole brain, balanced thinking). For effective communication—both sending and receiving—to occur, those engaged in dialogue must rationally and emotionally consider each other's background, culture, history, triggers, etc. When you have something important to say and in the process of saying it you trigger an emotional reaction, then rational-emotional balance is jeopardized and effective communication is put at risk.

So, it is ever so important to consider the receiver's interpretation and anticipate subsequent reactions to our choice of words, voice, and body language. If interpretation of what we see and hear (real or imagined) triggers an unintended emotional reaction, then all our prep work may be for naught. Even when the purpose of a communication is to evoke emotions, as in a Visionary/Dreamer leadership style, important conversations must be planned carefully. Knowing our audience is essential if our communication is to have the intended impact.

> The goal of communication is for the *receiver's impact*—
> what happens as a result—to match the *sender's*
> *intent*—what is desired out of the conversation.

Effective dialogue requires participants to understand as well as be understood—listening and talking are shared. Our impatience often gets in the way of good intentions and, as a result, our actions can trigger emotional responses. For example, suppose a friend of yours is excited to share stories from her vacation—a place where you recently vacationed. While she is talking, her stories flood your thinking with memories of your vacation; so, you jump in on the conversation and talk about what *you* did when you were there, what *you* saw, what *you*... What just happened? You hijacked the conversation. Rather than being interested and listening to her stories, you made the conversation about you. Hijacking a conversation leaves the recipient feeling unappreciated and angry; apparently, the hijacker places greater value on their vacation experiences than yours. Have you had your conversation hijacked? How did it make you feel? And you, do you hijack conversations?

COMMUNICATION STYLES

Communication styles can be *aggressive, passive, passive-aggressive,* or *open-direct* (see Figure 4.3) depending on how the message is communicated, which is often influenced by our underlying thoughts and emotions, the words we choose, how we say the words, and our body language. Unlike leadership styles, there is a preferred default style of communication. It is *open-direct:* **high** *respect for others' needs* and **high** *advocacy for one's own needs.*

Figure 4.3: <u>Communication Styles-Needs Matrix</u>

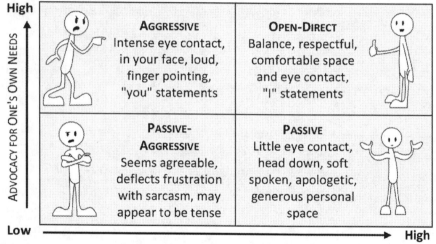

Over time, we each develop a specific *personal* communication style. The generic styles (above) are given nuances in meaning, expression, and sound based on our decisions (conscious and unconscious) about how to communicate. This is not necessarily how you always communicate, but it is a personal comfort style accompanied by a repertoire of communication behaviors and routines.

It is easy to understand how use of communication styles complement leadership styles; agreement of the two are necessary for authentic leadership. Suppose a workplace or family emergency occurs—chaos and confusion abound. A commanding leadership style (which is appropriate in an emergency, provides decisive direction) accompanied by an aggressive communication style gets your voice heard—appropriate given the circumstances. What would not work, and be inappropriate given the circumstances, is for you to inconspicuously walk in the room and in a soft voice, low presence, and with little to no eye contact, say, "Everyone, listen to me. We must…" Most people will not even notice you entered the room. Your delivery would be very understated. It would not be what you said, but how you said it, that would be a problem.

Passive style of communication - **high** *respect for others' needs* and **low** *advocacy for one's own needs*: Generally speaking, people using this style do not readily express their viewpoints, beliefs, or judgments. They tend to be quiet and calm, and tend not to talk much. When it is necessary to speak, it is often in a soft voice, even sounding apologetic. A passive communicator gives the impression of being introverted or shy: eye contact is limited or avoided, and body positioned to be less noticeable with generous personal space.

Since passive communicators do not readily express their opinions or feelings, their needs may not be identified or met. As a result, frustrations or annoyances can mount. Once passive communicators have reached their high tolerance threshold for unacceptable behavior, they are prone to volatile outbursts, which are usually out of proportion to the triggering incident. After the outburst, however, they often feel shame, guilt, and confusion.

Aggressive style of communication - **low** *respect for others' needs* and **high** *advocacy for one's own needs*: Generally speaking, people using this style forcefully state opinions or feelings. If an aggressive communicator is unsure if you heard what they had to say, what do they do? Say it again, but even louder. This style of communicator is not a good listener. An aggressive style of communication is about advocating their position; they do the talking, commonly interrupt, and talk over others. Emotions are strong with this style. Eye contact is fixed and staring—laser eyes. An aggressive communicator tends to be in your face, intruding on the receiver's personal space.

Since aggressive communicators express their feelings, state their opinions, or advocate for their needs while ignoring the needs of others, they may frustrate, offend, or alienate others. We often communicate aggressively when we are trying to exert power over others, get our voice heard, or feel threatened. Aggressive communication can sometimes have an accusatory tone or belittle the listener.

Passive-Aggressive style of communication - **low** *respect for others' needs* and **low** *advocacy for one's own needs*: This style is so named because both styles, passive and aggressive, occur at the same time: one on the inside, the other on the outside. Which style do you think occurs on the inside, passive or aggressive? That is right—aggressive. On the inside is a pressure cooker; they are about to explode. That is why we often see passive-aggressive communicators with their arms crossed, jaws tight, and lips pressed, as if they are containing pent-up emotions. If what is bottled-up on the inside got out, there would be trouble. Generally speaking, this communication style does not openly communicate anger or frustration; rather, they vent their feelings with sarcasm and facial expressions. They appear to be cooperative on the surface, but behind the scenes, they are likely to undermine efforts in an indirect way.

Passive-aggressive communicators appear passive but are really acting out anger. They often gesture a smile even though they are frustrated or angry. People who develop a pattern of passive-aggressive communication usually feel powerless, stuck, and resentful; in other words, they feel incapable of dealing directly with the object of their resentments. Instead, they express their anger by subtly undermining the object (real or imagined) of their resentments. We have seen this type of behavior before: someone fakes effort while clandestinely performing poorly to undermine a project's success.

Open-Direct style of communication - **high** *respect for others' needs* and **high** *advocacy for one's own needs*: This style is considered to be an effective default style because this communicator respectfully states their wants, needs, and expectations; they seek to understand and be understood. Generally speaking, they express feelings appropriately, use eye contact properly, convey respect for themselves and others, and respect personal space.

Open-direct communicators clearly state their opinions, express their feelings, or firmly advocate for their rights and needs without violating the rights of others. These individuals are strong advocates for themselves while being very respectful of the rights of others. Characteristics of an open-direct communicator are calm, confident, clear, and controlled.

Like leadership styles, it is often necessary to sequence or blend aspects of various communication styles in order to achieve a desired outcome. For example, a leader using an open-direct style may use aspects of an aggressive style (talking over others) or a passive style (soft spoken) to achieve a communication's aim. Aligning leadership and communication styles to meet specific individual, group, and environmental needs can greatly enhance individual and organizational success.

So, what are the descriptors (words, voice qualities, and body language) of each style? Use of personal space? Eye contact? Posture? Consider the messages each communication style sends as well as how might that style impact the receiver. Though leadership and communication styles have much in common, overuse of passive, aggressive, and passive-aggressive styles can have drawbacks. It can signal high or low *respect for others' needs* as well as high or low *advocacy for one's own needs*.

Take a few minutes to examine the communication styles. Think of 5-7 people that you have close relationships with; write their initials in the space provided in Figure 4.4. Then put each person's initials under the communication style that you **typically** use to communicate to that person. Examine your conversations carefully. Suppose most of your conversations to one of your close relationships goes like this: "WHERE'S THE REPORT." "GET ME THE INFORMATION." "DO YOUR WORK." The majority of what comes out of your mouth is an aggressive communication style. So, you would put that person's initials under the "Aggressive" column. Next, write the descriptors of each style (second row), then what messages each style send (third row), and finally how each style impacts the receiver (fourth row). If this exercise is helpful, use circled initials to indicate how each person responds back to you. In a perfect world, where will all the initials be? Open-direct. But, we do not live in a perfect world. Since we are

T. S. (Steve) Marshall, Ph.D.

often not as good at evaluating ourselves as we would like to be, consider eliciting feedback from the group of 5-7 people. What do you suppose their feedback results will be?

Figure 4.4: <u>Communication Style Matrix</u>
5-7 Close Relationships (Initials): 1._____, 2._____,
3._____, 4._____, 5._____,
6._____, 7._____

	Passive	Aggressive	Passive-Aggressive	Open-Direct
Initials				
What are the descriptors of this style (words, voice, body language)?				
What messages does this style send?				
How might this style impact the listener?				

Before we leave the topic of communication styles, I would like to briefly comment on the similarities and differences of passive and aggressive styles of communication, and introvert and extrovert learning styles. Though these communication and learning styles share some common characteristics, important differences exist. Observing interactions in a group of introverts and extroverts can be interesting. When in a group, introverts mostly process information internally; when they reach understanding, they will share it with the group. But, how do extroverts typically process information in a group? Externally: they process learning by thinking out loud—talking. So, while in the group, extroverts are wondering why those people, the introverts, are not participating in the discussion; and introverts are thinking if they, the extroverts, would shut up long enough to hear what they are saying, everyone would be better off. Both learning styles need to develop patience with the other, but do not confuse them with passive and aggressive styles. Both introverts and extroverts can (should) use all four communication styles.

Finally, let us go back to *hot buttons*, something that evokes an emotional response. It is important to keep the receiver focused on the message. When choosing your words, especially for important conversations, you need to be mindful of the provocative effect that some words can have on a receiver. "You" statements can be especially provoking—an emotional trigger that prompts a defensive response (*e.g.*, "You're always late."). "You" statements tend to be judgmental, place blame, and put the receiver on the defensive.

> If our aim is dialogue, then when composing your
> *thoughts and intentions*, do so in a means and manner
> that keeps the receiver focused on the message.

The opposite of a "you" statement is an "I" statement (see Figure 4.5). "I" statements keep the responsibility for thoughts, feelings, desires, and behaviors on the sender. Remember, no one can force you to feel a certain a way. So, instead of saying, "You're not keeping up with the work I'm giving you." Perhaps phrase it as, "I'm concerned about the completion of the work."

Figure 4.5: "You" and "I" Statements

"You" Statements	"I" Statements
You didn't explain that very well.	*I'm* having trouble understanding this.
You made me frustrated when...	*I* felt frustrated when...
You always critique my work.	*I* feel my work is not being understood clearly.

For critical conversations, there is an axiom that if you cannot rephrase or rewrite a "you" statement into an "I" statement, then perhaps it should not be said at all: "You're stupid." I can rewrite it as "I think you're stupid." No, that doesn't work either; perhaps it should not be said at all. Such statements are judgmental and can be threatening to the receiver. "You" statements often evoke an emotional response that leads to a disappointing back-and-forth argument: "You." "No, you." "No..." It is quite often that "you" statements are accompanied by finger pointing. And we wonder how the important conversation turned out so bad. *You can say what you mean without being mean when you say it.*

Even if the issue is conduct, you must choose your words carefully. Even then, it is not the receiver, but the receiver's behavior that needs to be addressed. The receiver is not the problem, but it is a particular behavior of the receiver that is detracting from effective performance. There is no "I" statement for conduct issues. If a person has a problem with being on time—tardiness—then it is not, "I'm sorry we are starting too early for you." The issue is the behavior relative to tardiness, and it needs to be addressed. Even so, no need to provoke an emotional response with a "you" statement.

LISTENING AND RESPONDING

Hearing requires little effort; it relies on ears. Listening requires considerable effort; it relies on balanced mental faculties and focused attention. As we have already seen, the sender bears a significant responsibility for the success of a communication: you have to plan your *thoughts and intentions*, determine the appropriate *format*, and *convey* your thoughts. The sender also shares responsibility for listening; that is, they must ensure the receiver is prepared to listen.

> For successful dialogue, both the sender and the receiver must commit to the conversation.

Too often, people tell me that they have coworkers, friends, etc., in their lives who do not listen to them. I am told, "They," those who are not listening, "have a big problem." Perhaps. But, for communication to be successful, we need to create an environment that enables people to listen. All parties to a conversation must be mentally prepared and focused to seek understanding and to be understood. When people *do not listen* to you, perhaps the reason is impatience—not theirs, but yours. Just because you, the sender, are ready to talk, does not mean that they, the receiver, are ready to listen. On several occasions, I have asked a sender if we could pause an important conversation because I was not able to give them my full attention. At that moment, competing priorities and timelines had my attentions divided; focused listening and effective dialogue was not going to happen.

A longtime client of mine likes to schedule most of our calls for when she is in the car driving; she has an hour-plus commute, each way, every day for work. She says driving is the best time for her to talk without the constant interruptions of the office. Though it is her preference, excessive vehicle and wind noise accompanied by fading signal strength makes listening difficult for both of us; having a quality conversation is truly a challenge. During these calls, I am usually at my desk with my full attention focused on listening and taking notes; she, on the other hand, is behind the wheel driving in traffic, so at best, her attention is divided. After our call, I always email her with my understanding of what we talked about and agreed to. The conversation, not the content, is a lot of work.

> Creating an environment for listening is essential
> when dialogue and understanding is critical.

When I have something really important that I want to discuss with my "behind the wheel" client, I will wait, as long as it is not time sensitive, until I am onsite. We will get out of the office—grab a coffee, and talk face-to-face. Yes, I could have another commute drive call, but when focused listening and understanding is crucial, face-to-face communication is best. When the message is important, I do not want to chance getting it wrong; so, I do everything I can to achieve the desired outcome. Face-to-face conversation, incorporating all the aspects of communication, enhances our chances of getting it right.

Rather than waiting, I could force a conversation across time zones, but knowing my client—my audience—she will be multi-tasking and her attention to our conversation would be divided. Divided attention is *not* what I want; so, when a conversation is important (and when it can wait), I too must be patient and prepare the receiver to listen. If I am **not** patient and **do not** prepare a receiver for listening, is a failed conversation the receiver's fault? No, at least not entirely. Dialogue does not just occur at *your* convenience, when *you* are ready, or when the timing suits *you*. For the last time, who in language determines if a communication is meaningful or not, the sender or receiver? The receiver. *A sender's impatience is not a receiver's fault.*

> Both the sender and receiver must be mentally prepared
> and focused for meaningful dialogue to occur.

So, to prepare an environment for listening, minimize or eliminate distractions and preoccupation—smart phones, social media, etc. It is helpful to schedule a conversation or ask if it is a good time to talk—know your audience. Perhaps the best time of the day to have an important conversation is not during peak hours of operation; during then, attentions are focused on service delivery, putting out fires, etc. Likewise, perhaps the best time of the evening to have an important conversation is not during the receiver's favorite program. Sure, if you asked, they would likely turn off the TV and attempt interest, but their attention would be divided by thoughts of what they are missing. Listening requires that you pay attention to the other person; it is hard to do that if distractions compete for your attention.

Consistent with healthy relationships, effective communication, managing emotional responses, and listening is how we respond to others when they share *good news* (or *positive experience*).[11] Think about it: when something amazing happens to you, what do you do? You look to share it with someone, not just anyone, but those people that you have special relationships with

---

[11] Shelly Gable, assistant Professor of Psychology at the University of California, has examined the different types of responses we give to other people's good new; active-constructive responding. Perceived Responses to Capitalization Attempts Scale. From Gable, E. L., Reis, H. T., Impett, E. A., & Asher, E. R., Capitalizing on Daily Positive Events, *Journal of Personality and Social Psychology, 87,* copyright © 2004.

and who are on your short list of people to call. Keep in mind that it *may not be good news* to the **receiver**, but it is *good news* to the **sender**. So, to maintain healthy relationships, responding positively to moments of joy and good news is the right thing to do. Granted, exceptions may exist, but showing authentic interest makes the sender feel valued and understood.

I had been working with the Regional Director of a multinational corporation for more than a year to modernize work processes, develop staff competencies, and dramatically improve workplace capabilities and performance. The director was an impressive leader with all the right stuff, truly a pleasure to work with. During the most critical phase of transition, implementation, and roll-out, he called to let me know that he accepted a senior corporate position and would be leaving at the end of the month. Oh my, I thought to myself. This project is his baby; how is his leaving going to affect project implementation and roll-out? Trying not to let my concerns for the project show in my voice, I expressed congratulations and excitement for his advancement: "Wow! I'm so happy for you. We need to find time during my next site visit for us to talk more so you can tell me all about it."

Though his promotion came at a bad time (project-wise), it was truly good news for him and the organization; responding upbeat and positively was the right thing to do. Work happens through relationships, and leadership is not only on our terms. The Regional Director's good news was not good news to the management team he was leaving behind to implement his vision. It took several days of working with the team to revise management roles and responsibilities, and restore confidences for the upcoming roll-out. During the next project meeting with the departing director, we were able to discuss project concerns, leadership roles, and multiple priorities without anyone becoming defensive or emotional.

If the management team would have responded negatively—emotionally—to the news of his promotion, the turmoil may have unraveled the whole project; it could have sidelined a year's worth of work. The project goal was not about the *who*—the Regional Director—but the *what*—moving regional capabilities and performance into the 21st century.

Because this understanding of *active, constructive responding* to other's good news and excitement is so critical to healthy relationships, effective communication, and leadership, I would like to share a couple of short examples: An excited coworker comes by your desk to share the good news of successfully completing their probation; your response: "Whatever." Your child comes home from school excited to tell you about something that happened in class; your response: "Not now. I'm busy." You get the idea.

Granted, there are times when you genuinely cannot drop everything to appropriately respond. At least respond civilly and let the sender know you will get right back to them as soon as you take care of what you are doing.

CHAPTER 5

MOTIVATION

I mentioned that I was a golfer; less so now, but there was a time when I was on the course every Saturday and most Sundays. For me, golf was more about hanging out with other people than the practice of the game; golf was a social outlet. For instance, I never golfed by myself; without someone to play with, golf was boring. The good thing about where we live is that you can play golf year-round. Though you can play, not everyone does; winter golf means walking for four-plus hours outside in the cold rain on a wet, soggy course—golf carts are often not allowed because the ground is too soft. People who saw us on the course that time of year must have thought we were crazy. Here is where motivation comes in: what would motivate a person to leave a warm, dry, comfortable bed to play golf in the cold, miserable rain? It was not the love of the game; it was a sense of belonging. In this chapter, we will examine motivators and demotivators, and the role of expectations in motivation.

Everyone has certain needs, and everyone is motivated by their desire to fulfill those needs. It was my desire to fulfill my need for social connection that got me out of bed winter weekends to play golf. This understanding is important: no one can motivate anyone to do anything. Yes, you can coerce someone into action, but motivation comes from a desire to fulfill personal needs; it comes from within.

An important part of leadership is to determine *what* motivates people. You have to know the *what* before you can know *how* to motivate someone to take willing *action* (see Figure 5.1). To motivate someone, we need to create an environment that encourages and enables motivation to grow and flourish. *Leaders do not move people; they influence movement.* Motivation means we have to know others' goals, drives, interests, and ambitions. Like leadership, motivation is not just about you; it is about others—influencing others to action. Even so, sometimes the one who needs motivating is us. I bet there are many things, important things, on your to-do list that you just cannot seem to get around to doing. We will talk about a couple of approaches to motivation that may help you to motivate others as well as yourself.

Figure 5.1: <u>Motivation Process</u>

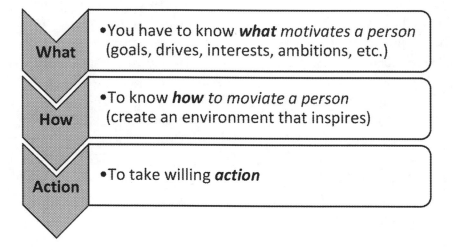

MOTIVATORS AND DEMOTIVATORS

In 1959, Frederick Herzberg introduced what he called the Two-Factor Theory[12] of motivation; namely, that two different factor groups must be present in order for sustained motivation to occur. One group is composed of factors that **motivate people** *when present*; another group of factors does not motivate anyone to do anything, but **demotivates people** *when*

---

[12] Herzberg's discussion of motivators and demotivators is worth reading: Herzberg, Frederick; Mausner, Bernard; Snyderman, Barbara B. (1959). *The Motivation to Work* (2nd ed.). New York: John Wiley.

they are absent. These two factor groups are independent of one another; a person can be highly motivated by what they do (their work), yet be very demotivated and dissatisfied by their working conditions (where they do it—safety, facilities) and whom they do it with (coworkers) and for (supervisors).

> **Motivators:** The presence of these motivates people: recognition, achievement, challenging work, responsibility, position, advancement, belonging, etc.[13] These factors are related to what an individual does—that is, to the nature of the work performed and with the capacity to gratify such needs as achievement, status, personal worth, and self-realization.

> **Demotivators:** The absence of these demotivates people: policies, administrative practices, job security, supervision, status, working conditions, interpersonal relations, and compensation. These factors do not motivate, but their absence leads to *demotivation* and dissatisfaction. For example, the presence of adequate compensation, good working conditions, and effective supervision does not motivate us—we expect these things; however, if we were paid pennies to go to work each day in a rundown building with a boss that yelled at us, I do not care how noble the cause, position, or praise, we would be demotivated to do the work—at least to do it well.

People are demotivated by an environment that is less than what they expect, but are seldom motivated by getting what is expected. People getting what they expect merely prevents them from being demotivated or dissatisfied. If motivation is what we seek, then we have to provide a whole other set of factors that motivate people (see Figure 5.2).

---

[13] McClelland discussed affiliation, achievement, and power as motivators to performance. More can be learned from: McClelland, David C., The Achieving Society (1961). University of Illinois at Urbana-Champaign's Academy for Entrepreneurial Leadership Historical Research Reference in Entrepreneurship.

Figure 5.2: <u>Motivation Factors</u>

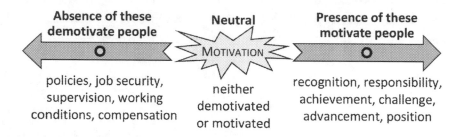

If a person lacks motivation, then we need to determine if it is due to them being demotivated (due to an absence of what is expected), or if it is due to them not being motivated (due to a lack of factors that motivates behavior).

> The prevention of demotivation is just as important
> as encouragement of motivation.

For example, it is unlikely that any of us has ever wrote a hotel a thank you note for providing clean linen on the bed or for having a working television; nor have we ever thanked restaurant management for giving us clean flatware. Why? We expect these things. THIS IS IMPORTANT: The presence of what we *expect* **does not motivate** us; we expect them, but their absence causes *demotivation* and dissatisfaction. What happens if our hotel room is not cleaned or the internet is not working, or we have dried food on a restaurant plate or a dirty napkin? We complain; such conditions are not what we expect. Getting what we expect merely prevents us from being demotivated or dissatisfied; it does **not** motivate or satisfy us. If a hotel or restaurant hopes to motivate us to come back, they need to rely on a whole set of other factors.

This concept of eliminating what *demotivates* before focusing on what *motivates* seems strange, but it is not all that uncommon or unnatural. Suppose you have a virus—sweats, aches and pains, sore throat, sneezing, headache, etc. Worried about you, your friends show up at your door with running gear. They think if they can just get you on your feet and take you on a run, you would feel so much better. No! When you are sick, what is needed is rest, not exertion. A run would make things worse, not better.

Let me ask this: once you are no longer sick, did your health improve? No, you merely restored your health to where it was before you got sick. Now that you are no longer sick and back to normal, if you want to improve your health, you have to do a whole other set of activities to do so (*e.g.*, diet and exercise). This understanding is important: eliminating the virus did not improve your health; it just got you back to normal. Once you are back to normal, if you want to improve your health, then diet and exercise is a good start. Likewise, *once you restore what demotivates someone, they are not motivated, just no longer demotivated; if you want to motivate them, then a whole other set of factors are needed.*

So, let us assume we have minimized or eliminated factors that *demotivate* performance and satisfaction—we are no longer sick. Now, let us move on to factors that motivate people, namely, recognition, achievement, challenging work, responsibility, position, advancement, belonging, and so on. A *sense of belonging* is what motivated me to play winter golf; a sense of belonging is why people, even when given the opportunity to telecommute, choose to commute to work. Belonging to an environment where people can talk and work with others can fulfill a core human need. Likewise, the need to belong is why some people join a committee, social group, or club.

A *sense of achievement* also motivates people—not achieving simple things nor impossible ones, but achieving realistic activities and tasks that when accomplished fulfill an important need. It is this sense of achievement that motivates people to learn a new language, develop a marketing campaign, or take on a new project. A *sense of position* can motivate people too. Role or position may include belonging to an occupation that serves society, such as being a police officer, firefighter, nurse, social worker, etc., as well as occupying an individual position of authority; both roles or positions can extend personal control or influence over people, events, or situations.

The point is, leaders have to know the *what* before they can know *how* to motivate someone to take *action*. It is by knowing someone—their needs, ambitions, etc.—that we can understand what floats their boat or lights their candle—what inspires them to action. If a person needs to *belong*, then create an environment that enables collaboration and teamwork. If *achievement* is the need, then structure work for them to make presentations, write procedures, or manage supplies. If it is *position*, then help them meet their needs by leading meetings, chairing committees, or making decisions that affect others.

EXPECTATION IN MOTIVATION

The role of expectation in motivation and satisfaction is important; expectations drift and must be regularly monitored and managed. About a decade ago, I was in Salt Lake City doing consulting work when my portable printer ran out of ink—not a problem since I always carry a backup. Unfortunately, that cartridge was my backup; so, I removed it from the printer, went to the hotel front desk, and asked them to call me a taxi to take me to the closest office supply store. "Oh, no," they said. "You don't need a taxi, we'll take you to the store, wait for you to get what you need, and then bring you back." Wow! That service surprised me; it also motivates me to this day to stay there whenever I am in Salt Lake City.

Here is the thing with expectation: I never knew that service existed, so I did not know to ask for it. But from that moment on, whenever I stayed at that hotel and needed to go somewhere, what did I do? I asked for it. After years of using the service, I no longer asked for it, I expected it. If the van service is not available, I complain. Our behavior is highly influenced by how reality meets expectations.

Expectations apply to people as well; just as leaders have expectations of staff, staff have expectations of leaders—hierarchical relationships. So, too, expectations exist among staff and among leaders—lateral or peer relationships. The danger with expectations is they can drift. When expectations and reality do not match up, mounting frustrations can undermine performance and morale. Expectations must be known, understood, and agreed upon, and must be regularly monitored to ensure they are realistic and achievable. On occasion, expectations may need to be reset; expectations can be unrealistic.

Leaders have to know the *what* before they can create the *how* to motivate people to take willing *action*. A leader's understanding of group and individual motivators and demotivators, as well as the role group and individual expectations play in motivation, is critical to achieving personal and organizational outcomes.

CHAPTER 6

CONFLICT RESOLUTION

With heightened security today, it is common for people to go through a TSA-style screening to gain access to federal and corporate buildings. Your name must be on the visitors list before you and your items are screened; then, often, you must wait for your point-of-contact to escort you to their office. It is a sad but necessary security measure of our time. Due to the nature of one client's work, they have armed guards processing access into the building, and then armed staff that escort visitors to their destination. During one of my visits, the client told me of a conflict that occurred between a guard who grants access to the building and an armed staff member. The dispute regarded the location of a particular customer stanchion post—the ones with retractable belts used for customer wait lines. Most guards and staff knew of the tension between the two and chuckled about the silliness of their dispute. Well, the conflict escalated one day when one of the two—my client was unsure which one—moved the stanchion and marked its location on the floor with a felt-tip marker. Observing this, the other person walked to the stanchion and kicked it off its spot. At that point, two grown men, with guns, got into a physical confrontation in the customer lobby. Oh my! When emotion trumps reason, emotional self-control, rational thinking, and effective communication become difficult.

Another client told me of a confrontation between her husband and a new neighbor that resulted in a police response. It started when the new neighbors let their yard go, then they began leaving their garage door open all day and night, and it peaked when the neighbor's husband began parking his truck in front of their house. What got her husband so upset was that there was plenty of room in the neighbor's own driveway to park their truck; better yet, if they cleaned the junk out of their garage, they could park their vehicles inside and close the garage door. Frustrated, the client told me her husband began parking his car in front of their own house, instead of in their garage, to deny the neighbor from parking there. Unfortunately, a gap in his timing resulted in the neighbor's truck being parked once again in front of their house; this time, it stayed there for days. In retaliation, her husband began parking his car in front of the neighbor's house. What a mess! Since the street is public property, nothing governed the parking of vehicles on it. My client told me that during this entire time, neither husband spoke to the other, until one day the two faced off in the street resulting in a police response. When emotions flare, things can deteriorate fast. To those in the throes of conflict, it is always the other person's behavior, the other's actions, that is at fault. In the eyes of the beholder, they are a victim whose actions are justified.

Not all conflict is between two or more people or groups. Sometimes, conflict is internal; we can have mixed feelings. For example, one of your subordinates comes into your office and says, "My child is very ill. I want to resign from my job." In this instance, the person is conflicted between the need to be home with his/her child and the need to be at work. Perhaps their job provides the only means to care for the child. If they quit, then it may cause more harm than good. When people are in conflict (or conflicted), the presence of heightened emotions may result in a diminished ability to think clearly, rationally. So, a person, like the parent with the sick child, *may* realize they are not thinking clearly and seek the help of someone who can provide reasonable insight, balanced thinking, and sound judgment to their issue. In this chapter, we will examine the principles and process for resolving conflict.

Conflict is an emotional state; it is a state of unresolved difference or unresolved feelings within an individual, two or more people, or groups. Conflict often occurs when people disagree on an issue that *threatens* their respective goals, values, or needs. When feelings are *threatened*, it can *trigger an emotional response* that affects our ability to view and approach a situation in an objective, rational manner. Given the state of mind of a person in conflict, especially in a heightened state of conflict, reasonable solutions to a problem seem limited. As a result, very smart people can do very dumb things when emotions get the better of them. *When emotions increase, rational thinking decreases.* Conflict can trigger the same adrenaline threat response and diminished mental faculties described in Chapter 3.

> People in conflict normally perceive what they
> see and hear emotionally, not rationally.

We would all agree that the first two conflict scenarios are not the result of a balanced mental state. Unfortunately, unresolved conflict can result in poor choices—neither scenario should have gone that far. *Knowing you* as well as *knowing others* is a core leadership competency. What signals does your body send you when you feel conflict? Does your heart pound, palms sweat, face turn red, mouth get dry, etc.? Train yourself to recognize the symptoms of conflict in you, as well as to read them in others.

Given that conflict tends to be emotionally charged, it requires a process for resolution that acknowledges and accounts for participants' heightened emotional state (see Figure 6.1). If people in conflict had balanced mental states, then their issue would be addressed using a decision making or problem solving process; they could reasonably discuss the issue at hand.

Figure 6.1: <u>Peoples State of Mind</u>

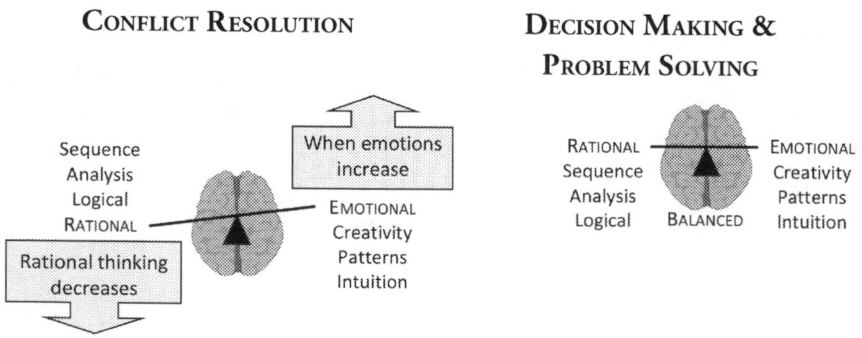

PRINCIPLES FOR RESOLVING CONFLICT

Since conflict is emotional and few know how to resolve it in a constructive fashion, most people avoid it. Generally, it is *better to deal with conflict than to ignore it*, especially if we can approach the process positively. Two key principles for resolving conflict are:

➤ **Disclosing information** about how you see yourself, the other person, and the conflict you are experiencing; sharing your perceptions and your reasoning about the situation; asking for what you want; and

➤ **Listening** includes using active listening skills to understand the other person, asking questions, and receiving information in a way that is non-judgmental.

Unfortunately, the very two principles required to resolve conflict are the least likely things to occur in conflict. For example, Chris and Lee have been cubicle mates for months. Every workday, the two of them sit in a small work area and share common office items. Unfortunately, Chris harbors a deep dislike for Lee, and it has been intensifying the past couple of weeks. The sound of Lee's voice, her giggle, and even the sight of her now makes him sick. Chris cannot take it any longer. It has gotten so bad that Chris does not even want to come to work. So, he brings the supervisor a note from his doctor; it states that the glare from the windows is giving him headaches and that he needs to move. "Perfect," the supervisor says. "I've been waiting to move you and Lee." "No!" Chris thinks, "What now?"

Disclosing information is the last thing Chris is going to do. He cannot go to his supervisor and tell her the real reason he wants to move; it would sound so childish and petty. So, he creates an elaborate story, even contrives symptoms to receive a doctor's note, all to get away from Lee. People in conflict commonly create proxy or surrogate stories that sound quite noble on the surface, but in actuality are cover stories for something else—perhaps a deeper, less noble reason. Recall the subordinate with the very ill child who wanted to resign? Well, the speculation is the child is quite well and the subordinate was hoping the storyline would gain him/her favor in receiving one of the precious few telework positions in the upcoming schedule. Wow!

If this is indeed so, then there is no conflict here, at least not one regarding the child; rather, it is a subordinate conduct issue. Like in the Wizard of Oz, when it comes to conflict, it is important to look behind the curtain—what is the real story? The *tales* parties tell you regarding conflict may be just that, tales (subjective and biased); they may not be *facts* at all. We have all been there: when conflict happens, everyone rushes to tell us the *facts*. Yes, but the *facts according to whom*? The following quotes may answer that question: "There are three sides to every story. Yours. Mine. What really happened: the truth" (Jeyn Roberts); and "Listening to both sides of a story will convince you that there is more to the story than both sides" (Frank Tyger).

Watch for **position vs. interest**. *Position* is what a person is asking for—often presented as what a person "wants." Positions are firm demands. *Interest* is the reason behind the person's position: the needs, concerns, and values that motivate the person. Interests are composed of the wants, needs, desires, and concerns that motivate people.

As for *listening*, well, do you think people in conflict are good listeners? No. Listening requires mental balance—rational and emotional thinking. As we discussed, effective dialogue requires participants to understand as well as be understood; listening and talking are shared. Given the emotional state of conflict, the brain is not prepared for listening—emotions create too much interference.

CONFLICT RESOLUTION PROCESS

The conflict resolution process follows the I-D-E-A-L model. If successful, conflict resolution can deepen parties' understanding of circumstances and each other, and build group cohesion. Understandably, the discussion needed to resolve conflict expands people's awareness of the situation and gives them insight into how they can achieve their own goals without undermining those of other people. When conflict is resolved effectively, the parties involved can develop stronger mutual respect and a renewed faith in their ability to work together. Finally, conflict pushes participants to examine their goals in close detail, understand the things that are important to them, and enhance their effectiveness.

The I-D-E-A-L conflict resolution process follows. Try it; use the worksheet on the bottom right to work through one of your own conflicts.

Identify and *Describe* are usually completed before meeting with the parties together—analyze the situation.

➢ **I - <u>Identify</u> and understand the problem**: Take as much time as you need to understand the *real problem*. Think back to what we discussed in Chapter 3; namely, our response to what we see and hear is not based on what actually happened—*the facts*; rather it is based on our interpretation of what happened—*the tale* we tell ourselves. Do not rush to resolve what is stated—perhaps the tale is a diversion or symptom of the problem; instead, endure to find the root cause of the problem— the real reason for the conflict. For example, if conflict occurs due to over scheduling of interview rooms, even if you resolve this instance of conflict, it will happen again because you have not resolved the root cause of the problem—over scheduling of interview rooms. Identify the real problem and understand it as it actually exists (the facts) as well as how it is perceived to exist (the tales) by the parties.

> I-D-E-Λ-L CONFLICT RESOLUTION
>
> I: _____
> _____
> D: _____
> _____
> E: _____
> _____
> A: _____
> _____
> L: _____
> _____

➢ **D - <u>Describe</u> the problem**: Though the conflict is emotional— subjective and biased—try to describe the situation as objectively and accurately as possible. Follow the journalistic or investigative method of inquiry and learn *who, what, when, where,* and *how.* Be specific in your account of the event and minimize parties' exaggerations—just the facts.

Express, Ask, and *List* commonly take place with all parties present; participants become problem solvers who together seek an efficient and amicable outcome—mutual gain.

> ➢ **E - Express** your concerns and how you feel: Use "I" rather than "you" statements (elements of an open-direct communication style discussed in Chapter 4), and, again, minimize exaggeration.
> ➢ **A - Ask** for their perspective and reasonable change: Use "what" and "how" questions, not "why" questions. Repeat back what you heard to check your understanding. Work towards a win-win resolution.
> ➢ **L - List** the positive impact of resolution: Describe the positive outcomes once conflict is resolved. Avoid focusing on negative consequences.

Resolving conflict is a critical leadership and life skill, and it is often better to resolve conflict sooner than later; rarely does it fade away on its own. So, plan your communication carefully and be mindful that those in conflict have heightened sensitivity to use of words, tone of voice, and body language. Moreover, it is ever so important not to get sucked into the drama. Stay neutral, above the fray and emotions. Though resolving conflict and communication in conflict are both difficult, the consequence of not addressing and resolving it can be worse. Objectivity, discipline, and patience usually lead to mutually agreeable outcomes.

CHAPTER 7

DECISION MAKING

We make thousands of decisions of varying importance and in varying environments every day. But, experience suggests that many of us are not as good as we think we are at making good decisions. Sure, making decisions is easy; but, making good ones requires a solid understanding of the decision making process. Some basics in strategic thinking, planning, and accountability are helpful too.

While the vast majority of day-to-day decisions are routine, involving little uncertainty or risk, others are not be so easy—they can be complicated and full of uncertainty and risks. Furthermore, decision makers must constantly wrestle with the competing and conflicting realities within the greater organizational context, in both upstream and downstream processes, and between internal and external influences. Decision making (at work, home, and elsewhere) can be complicated—getting it *right* in one area may cause *havoc* in another. In this chapter, we will examine the process for making sound decisions and communicating the decision.

Decision making and *problem solving* share like process paths (see Figure 7.1) and are often used interchangeably with reference to a situation, problem, or issue. Do not get wrapped up in terminology or over think one or the other. Just stay focused on the matter at hand. Even so, *decision making* and *problem solving* have their distinctions:

> **Decision Making**: typically refers to a "situation." The purpose of decision making is to make *a choice*—may or may not result from a problem.

> **Problem Solving**: typically refers to a "problem." The purpose of problem solving is to *find a solution*—may or may not result in a decision.

Figure 7.1: Decision Making & Problem Solving Model

These two processes, though distinct, will collectively be referred to as *decision making* because good problem solving involves consideration of more than just one potential solution. Thus, a decision among potential solutions to a problem must be made—which *solution* will best solve the problem.

The decision-making process starts with becoming aware of a situation and ends with a decision. Defining the situation is critical for a successful outcome. The process diverges to explore many possibilities and converges on the best idea—the decision. Decision making requires making a choice—a deliberate action—with imperfect information in imperfect environments, which exposes us to risks and consequences, in order to achieve an outcome. Naturally, to decide one must have the authority to make the decision.

The first priority in decision making is to determine *what is to be decided*—the situation—and *who is deciding it*—who owns the situation/problem. Know your turf: do not make decisions that are not yours to make. This helps cuts down on disagreement about situation definition, requirements, criteria, and outcomes. If needed, consult management and stakeholders, and get help from facilitators and data analysts.

Perfect decisions are rare—seek effective ones.

As the process unfolds, keep in mind that decision makers, decision information, and the environment we work in are all imperfect. Too often people never get around to deciding because they are constantly in search of *perfect*. Reluctance to decide is different from an inability to decide. One of the primary reasons people drag their feet in decision making is fear or anxiety of making the wrong decision. If a decision is truly needed and the timing is imminent, then one must have the courage to make a decision and see it through. Sadly, pressures of personal and professional fallout from making a wrong decision can cause some decisions to be avoided or postponed indefinitely. The exception to postponing a decision applies to *emotional decisions*; take *time out* to deal with anger, hurt, etc.—get the facts and then decide. Finally, keep in mind that decision making must be resourced. Available resources, to include people's time, are important considerations. High ambitions are fine, but without sufficient time and budget, there is little hope for success.

MAKING SOUND DECISIONS

There is no magic formula for effective decision making, but a realistic, rational method for making sound decisions is shown in Figure 7.2. The five-step Decision Making Cycle shows a practical approach that is flexible and accommodates different styles and challenges. These steps have long been recognized in decision making. Though it is convenient to show these steps in sequence, the process is iterative with multiple feedback loops. It is common to start, stop, go back, start again, stop... At the end of this chapter, there is a step-by-step example of applied decision making.

Figure 7.2: <u>Decision Making Cycle</u>

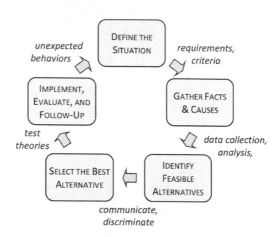

<u>Define the Situation</u>: Einstein said you cannot solve a problem until you define it. Yes, that is good advice. This is a critical first step because how one defines a situation influences how one determines causes and where one searches for solutions. Do not rush this step. An incorrectly stated or poorly framed situation can result in a poor decision. Especially here, it is critical to know whose sandbox you are playing in because decision information, requirements, criteria, alternatives, values, preferences, and much more may be greatly influenced by the decision maker.

Some key questions to consider: What is the decision situation? Does it warrant attention? Who is the decision maker? What are the decision requirements? What are the selection criteria? What is the desired result? What is the timeframe/urgency? What are the key assumptions and influences? Who would be good decision team members? Are skills, time, commitment, and resources sufficient?

Within this step, we must determine requirements, criteria, and key assumptions regarding the decision situation. *Requirements* are absolute—musts; requirements do not determine what is recommended, just what is eligible for recommendation. It is common for a decision maker to mandate minimal acceptable requirements that a decision must meet. Selection *criteria* allow people to discriminate among feasible alternatives to select the best recommendation. It is not unusual for selection criteria to conflict (*e.g.*, accuracy and timeliness). When this happens, no need to resolve the conflict or prioritize. If in doubt, define what constitutes the requirement and criteria—operational definitions or examples may be necessary. If acceptance and implementation of a recommendation is based on *key assumptions*, then they should be considered in the decision process. Finally, if you are the decision maker, then identifying requirements and criteria (in concert with organizational purpose, alignment, etc.) is your job; if you are not the decision maker, then there is no harm in proposing some.

A client told me she had 207 applicants that met the minimal job requirements for a professional position. She regretted the hours she and her staff had to spend to narrow the list. Once again, requirements discriminate; they are absolutes; they either include or exclude. For example, let us examine the decision requirements and criteria for Miss America. *Requirements* do not determine who is Miss America, just who is eligible to be Miss America.[14] Without requirements, anyone in the world could be Miss America. Each requirement includes or excludes participants in the candidate pool—that is the purpose of requirements. Criteria are then used to select Miss America from eligible contestants.

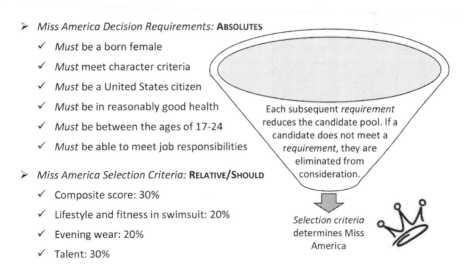

➤ *Miss America Decision Requirements:* **ABSOLUTES**

    ✓ *Must* be a born female

    ✓ *Must* meet character criteria

    ✓ *Must* be a United States citizen

    ✓ *Must* be in reasonably good health

    ✓ *Must* be between the ages of 17-24

    ✓ *Must* be able to meet job responsibilities

Each subsequent *requirement* reduces the candidate pool. If a candidate does not meet a *requirement*, they are eliminated from consideration.

➤ *Miss America Selection Criteria:* **RELATIVE/SHOULD**

    ✓ Composite score: 30%

    ✓ Lifestyle and fitness in swimsuit: 20%

    ✓ Evening wear: 20%

    ✓ Talent: 30%

Selection criteria determines Miss America

---

[14] Please pardon the use of this example, but it is one that most people are familiar with, and it clearly illustrates requirements and criteria. To the point of requirements, Miss Delaware (2014) was stripped of her title by Miss America organizers for being "too old"; she exceeded the age requirement during her term. Requirements include and exclude!

Like in the above example, criteria are commonly weighted. Criteria weighting is determined by the decision maker or may be established through expert judgment. Though criteria weighting should be normalized to 100%, other methods (scale of 1-5, 1-10, 1-100) can be effective.

In the client's case of 207 eligible applicants, their requirements were too few and too general—most everyone made it through the funnel. They had only two requirements: no felony conviction and a two-year degree. More requirements easily could have been added for this professional position. Perhaps, they could narrow the candidate pool by revising the existing education requirement: four-year degree with eight years' experience in a related field. If needed, clearly state assumptions about job programs, etc.

Once you have defined *what is being decided*, identified *who is deciding it*, and have come to agreement on *requirements, criteria,* and *key assumptions* (if any), it is necessary to consider *how to approach the decision making process*. We are not just interested in making the right decision, but the best one. If you decided on your own without others' input, will the decision be supported? If not, your decision will likely die in implementation. So, given what we know about the decision situation and the implementation environment, what is the best approach to arrive at a decision that will be both supported and successfully implemented? You decide, get input and you decide, or let others decide.

> We are not just interested in making the right decision, but the best one—one that can be supported and implemented.

Granted, sometimes a situation can be so pressing that you must make a decision, ready or not. It may not be possible to postpone the decision. Where appropriate, do your best to reach consensus. It is generally agreed that the informed few can produce better decisions than the informed one. Realize that others' decision-making styles, methods, and approaches may be different from yours. Personalities, thinking types, and communication styles vary too. So, be flexible, open-minded, and considerate of others. Keep in mind that decisions often involve more than objective criteria; they involve feelings. *Advantages of involvement* include expanded expertise, buy-in, and expanded perspectives. *Disadvantages of involvement* include conflict, frustration, and the consumption of time.

Usually, it is best for you to *decide alone* when it is an emergency, the outcome affects only the decision maker, when one person has all of the relevant information, or when one person is especially trusted to make a good decision. Usually, *consensus* is best when decisions have large ramifications, affects a lot of people, or decision making groups are small. Regardless, a rich exchange of ideas, whether in person, by phone, etc., can greatly enhance a decision outcome.

Gather Facts & Causes: It is very important to attest to the credibility of what you show and tell, and assess the credibility of what you are shown and told. Too often people take data and analysis for granted—because Excel did it, it must be right. Data, analysis, and its resulting information must be accurate and its integrity never be in question. When it comes to data, there are always special circumstances and context that are unknown to us. Even so, we should represent data and present information honestly and with good intentions. In other words, we should never deceive others or mask what is reasonably known. Data quality and credibility are directly connected to effective decision making. If the process of managing data is questionable, then judgments and recommendations based on it will also be questionable. Take your time and do it right. When it really matters, do not act hastily.

> Analysis of data should stimulate discussion,
> not itself be the subject of discussion.

Make sure you ask the right questions. Brainstorm questions before you start the fact and cause finding process. Consider some key questions: Have you confirmed the data? Do the numbers add up? Are all the totals there? Any grammatical or spelling errors? Have they been corrected? Are the analysis, findings, and message consistent? Is use and application of methodology consistent? What databases are available? What steps in the methodology are based on judgment? Whose judgment? What has worked and not worked in the past? Barriers/obstacles? What has been done before?

What do we know about it? Context? Who has been involved in past decisions in like situations? Experiences?

Keep in mind that good judgment is needed for collected data to yield reliable information. One must determine how much time is reasonable for gathering facts and causes. Naturally, the magnitude and urgency of the decision situation will greatly influence what is reasonable. Before you move on, make sure you step back and look at what you have gathered. Does it make sense? Also, be aware of biases, filters, and paradigms; they can influence the collection of reliable data and subsequent analysis of it.

If you are collecting data for the first time, include data from the past as well as the present, to the degree possible. This provides a *baseline* for assessing current information and demonstrating future improvements. It is difficult to set realistic goals and determine trends before baseline information is available. It is also a good idea to *test* your theory for collecting good data. Gather a small amount of data, then check to see if you are getting the data you need. Good data collection is essential for what follows—analysis and interpretation. All the tools and analysis will be of little help without good data. During this phase, it is common for other people to be involved in the data collection, so closely monitor the process. Do not assume everything is going according to plan—follow up.

A good strategy for collecting data should provide answers to these questions (commonly referred to as the journalistic or investigative method of data collection):

- ➤ **Why** is the data needed?
- ➤ **Who** will collect the data?
- ➤ **What** data will be collected?
- ➤ **When** will the data be collected?
- ➤ **Where** will the data be collected?
- ➤ **How much** data will be needed?
- ➤ **How often** will the data be collected?
- ➤ **How long** will the data be collected?
- ➤ **How** will the data be recorded and organized?

Though numbers, statistics, tables, and charts seem to be everywhere, conveying meaningful information with them can be elusive. To mean something, data must be presented in a manner to be of value to the decision maker. So, rather than talking to the data, reciting what people can see already, provide decision makers with information that lets the data speak to them. Data analysis and interpretations should provide decision makers with information regarding what happened, is happening, and is likely to happen; when, where, and why it did happen (causation); context and perspective (the story behind the numbers); and significance, importance, and relevance of the findings (who cares?). The presence of reliable data will not guarantee success; however, the resulting analysis and interpretation of meaningful data will enhance the likelihood that the resulting decision will achieve desired outcomes.

Identify Feasible Alternatives: Decisions are only as good as the alternatives—garbage in, garbage out. To be deemed an alternative, it must, as a minimum, meet decision requirements. Unless you are sifting through a list of known alternatives, creative thinking will be essential in this step. Brainstorming can be a useful technique to generate ideas that you later accept, reject, or combine as appropriate.

Good recommendations (alternatives) are something that meets requirements, satisfies as many criteria as possible, aligns with the organizational mission and goals, has a direct impact on performance, and has a defined scope, dedicated resources, realistic schedule, and consensus of understanding. Alternatives should be feasible, genuine, and sufficiently numerous. Generating alternatives is easy, but it is quite something else to generate good ones. Bad alternatives force one to choose among the lesser of evils. Feasible alternatives generally vary in their ability to satisfy selection criteria. Ultimately, feasible alternatives must be value added to customers, the organization, management, unions, employees, etc.

Select the Best Alternative: What constitutes best must be defined by criteria. Best does not necessarily mean good; it is relative: $1,000 fine or two days in jail? Neither is good. Some alternatives should never be selected and implemented; just because they make a list does not mean they are worth doing. Do not waste your time and resources on alternatives that are unlikely of success—some alternatives are worthy of consideration, others not. Eliminate those unworthy of consideration.

Reevaluate the top-ranked alternatives against defined criteria; if necessary, use selection criteria to narrow the list. Decision makers frequently face multiple and conflicting criteria. As a result, different criteria may lead to a different decision. So, take a break, clear your head, and then decide. Ask: Does the selection make sense? Are you comfortable with likely outcomes? Once a selection is made, it is time to implement it—decide and act. If you fail to implement the decision, it was all for naught.

The job of the selection criteria is to discriminate among feasible alternatives. Criteria may be qualitative and/or quantitative and may be weighted in importance—all may not be equal. It guides the process of selecting an alternative (see Figure 7.3).

Figure 7.3: <u>Decision Making Process Flow</u>

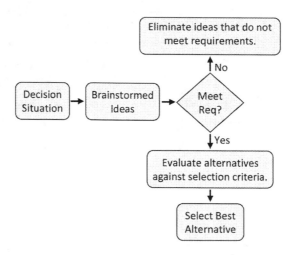

The true test is to ask the question, "If an otherwise good alternative does not meet the requirement, should it be dismissed or considered?" If the answer is to dismiss the alternative, this is truly a requirement (absolute). If, however, the answer is to consider the alternative as is, then the requirement must be changed or rewritten as a criteria. Selection criteria are relative and, as such, are negotiable desirables.

If an alternative does not meet a requirement, there are three things we can do: discard the alternative, change the requirement to include the alternative, or restate the requirement to a criteria. For example, if a requirement is *Must cost less than $8,000.00* and a candidate item costs $8,005.00, it must be **discarded**—it does not meet the requirement. Or, we can **change** the requirement: *Must cost less than $10,000.00*; now, what was once excluded is included. Or, we can **restate** the requirement and make it a criteria: *Cost*. In this instance, less cost is better than more cost—nothing is eliminated. Technically, I guess there is one more thing you can do: replace requirements and criteria all together with an **assumption** that the decision outcome will be affordable. It may take one or two test passes to sort out requirements and selection criteria. Then, select the best alternative based on well-thought-out decision requirements and criteria.

IMPLEMENT, EVALUATE, AND FOLLOW UP:

Making a decision can be liberating, but we have to live with the ones we make—being accountable. If we acknowledge problems when they arise and deal with them—learn from them—then we can hopefully avoid repeating like mistakes. On occasion, a well-intended decision that has a big payoff for one unit (upstream) may have dire consequences to another unit (downstream). Our aim is **not** to maximize the benefit of one area at the expense of another. Accountability refers to being responsible for one's decisions. Good decision making is served by transparency and having a variety of voices heard. Before you implement a decision, allow key staff and others to scrutinize the decision and your implementation plan, then test it on a small scale. There is always something worthwhile discovered through testing—decision makers cannot be expected to know everything. After testing, apply what you have learned regarding decision quality and implementation to enhance success.

To implement the alternative means to put it into action; namely, *plan the work, and work the plan*—follow up to make sure it gets done. The process is not complete until the decision is implemented. If you do not implement the decision, the decision has no value; it was a waste of resources. Your decision implementation plan should address resources, accountabilities, timetable, etc. If you are not good at planning the decision implementation, find someone who is. The purpose of the decision making process is to implement a carefully planned decision. The purpose of the implementation plan is to enhance implementation success. Use measures to monitor performance and follow up to ensure the decision has its intended outcome. Keep in mind that good decisions do not guarantee good outcomes, but it helps.

APPLIED DECISION MAKING EXAMPLE

Replacement vehicles for a motor pool fleet.

DEFINE THE SITUATION: Need two replacement vehicles for the motor pool fleet. Current vehicles are getting old, no longer suited for use, and not cost-effective. Need to replace two fleet vehicles with newer, more spacious, more economical, and more fuel-efficient vehicles. Fleet vehicle replacement *requirements*, *selection criteria*, and *assumptions* are shown in Figure 7.4.

Figure 7.4: *Decision Requirements, Selection Criteria, and Assumptions*

Decision Requirements - Absolutes/Musts	*Selection Criteria* - Relatives/Shoulds
• Vehicle *must* be made in USA. • Vehicle *must* seat at least four adults, but no more than six adults. • Vehicle *must* cost no more than $32,000.00. • Vehicle *must* be new and the current model year.	• Maximize passenger room • Maximize passenger safety • Maximize fuel efficiency • Maximize reliability • Minimize investment cost

Key Assumptions:
• Fleet vehicles are operated by different drivers and are subject to accelerated wear.
• Fleet vehicle drivers generally do not exercise the same care for fleet vehicles as they do for their own personal vehicles.

<u>Note</u>: The definition of the situation dictates the requirements. For example, requirements, selection criteria, and key assumptions would likely differ if they were for a family car. Other decision requirements and selection criteria may be appropriate, but these will suffice for this example.

GATHER FACTS/CAUSES: Since drivers generally do not exercise the same care for fleet vehicles as they do for their own personal vehicles—a key assumption—reliability is a chief concern. Vehicle safety is also paramount. Though the fleet is aging, maintenance records indicate normal wear-and-tear.

Operational Definitions: Requirements and selection criteria, as needed, are defined to assure shared understanding of what is being sought. Numbers in bold and parentheses represent weighting; weighting varies according to the situation. Since *safety* and *reliability* are "paramount" and "of chief concern," they are rated **10**, the highest possible rating on a 1-10 scale.

Operational definitions and weighting of selection criteria

Maximize Passenger Room (5): Based on the combined rear seat leg and shoulder room.

Maximize Passenger Safety (10): Based on the total number of stars awarded by the National Highway Traffic Safety Administration for head-on and side impact.

Maximize Fuel Efficiency (7): Based on the EPA fuel consumption for city driving.

Maximize Reliability (10): Based on the reliability rating given each vehicle by a consumer product testing company.

Minimize Investment Cost (9): Based on the purchase price.

T. S. (Steve) Marshall, Ph.D.

<u>Note</u>: If it were necessary, we would have operational definitions for requirements as well.

WHAT VEHICLES DO THE REQUIREMENTS ELIMINATE?

Requirement 1: *Eliminates* cars not manufactured in the USA.

Requirement 2: *Eliminates* vans, buses, and sports cars.

Requirement 3: *Eliminates* higher-end luxury cars, those costing more than $32,000.00.

Requirement 4: *Eliminates* used cars and models not of the current year.

Despite the limitations imposed by the decision requirements, four possible fleet replacement vehicles (decision alternatives) were identified. They are the following vehicles: Arrow, Bullet, Cruiser, and Dart.

	Arrow	*Bullet*	*Cruiser*	*Dart*
Made in USA?	Yes	Yes	Yes	Yes
Seats 4-6?	Yes	Yes	Yes	Yes
Costs <$32,000?	Yes	Yes	Yes	Yes
New Vehicle?	Yes	Yes	Yes	Yes

Vehicle Alternatives (columns); Requirements (rows)

<u>Note</u>: As you can see, identifying alternatives in this example was simply a matter of elimination; vehicles that did not meet the requirements were removed from consideration. Little to no creative thinking or brainstorming of alternatives was required.

Data regarding each vehicle were compiled according to each alternative and criteria.

Vehicle Alternatives

Selection Criteria		Arrow	Bullet	Cruiser	Dart
	Room:	86 inches	88 inches	80 inches	89 inches
	Safety:	14 Starts	17 Stars	15 Stars	19 Stars
	Fuel Efficiency:	21 mpg	19 mpg	22 mpg	21 mpg
	Reliability:	80 rating	70 rating	65 rating	85 rating
	Cost:	$31,000	$26,000	$22,000	$29,000

SELECT THE BEST ALTERNATIVE:

Option 1: PROS AND CONS

ARROW	
Pros	**Cons**
good fuel efficiency	fewest safety stars
2nd best reliability	highest cost

BULLET	
Pros	**Cons**
2nd most room	worst fuel efficiency
2nd in safety	

CRUISER	
Pros	**Cons**
best fuel efficiency	least room
lowest cost	3rd in safety stars
	worst reliability

DART	
Pros	**Cons**
most room	
best safety	
good fuel efficiency	
best reliability	

CONCLUSION: Since *safety* and *reliability* are rated the most important criteria, the Dart appears to be the best alternative. The Dart scores pros in other criteria as well. The Dart has four advantages and no disadvantages. So, the Dart *seems* to be the best alternative. The Dart also meets all the requirements and solves the problem.

Option 2: Matrix (Weighted – 10 point scale)

Weight / Rating	Room (5)		Criteria Weight / Fuel Efficiency (7)		Reliability (10)		Cost (9)		TOTAL
ARROW	6	30	5 / 9	63	6	60	5	45 / **31**	248
BULLET	Rating / 45	Weighted Rating	8	56	7	70	8	72 / 40	323
CRUISER	4		10	70	5	50	10	90 / 35	290
DART	10	50	10 / 100	9 / 63	10	100	6	54 / 45	367

CONCLUSION: The Dart meets all the requirements, best satisfies selection criteria, and arrives at the best decision.

Compiling decision information on a summary worksheet can be very useful. An example of such a worksheet follows:

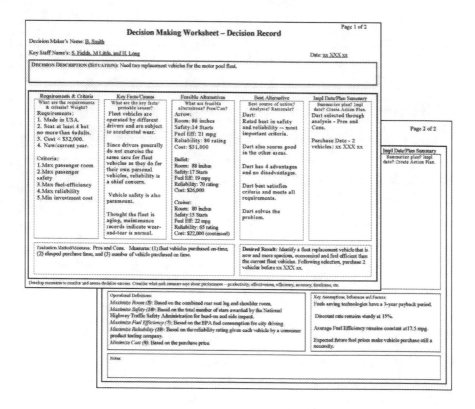

COMMUNICATING THE DECISION

Whatever you do, do not let a good decision suffer from ineffective or incomplete communication. It is important to communicate both the decision and reason behind it. Plan your communication (*e.g.*, face-to-face, staff meeting, public meeting, e-mail, etc.) and check understanding of the message—did they get it? Outline key decision points ahead of time. Demonstrate how the decision is aligned with and supports organizational goals, objectives, etc. Be your own devil's advocate.

Communicating the decision should be short and to the point. Treat communicating the decision like a guerilla raid—get in and get out. Too many people (and decision teams) spend up to an hour or longer parading people and presenting PowerPoint slide after slide—help! Before you start, know your audience, their background, and decision context. A useful—brief and effective—presentation structure follows:

The decision situation we were resolving was: _____

_____

The situation came to our attention because: _____

_____

_____

Investigation revealed (leading facts/causes): _____

_____

_____

    After extensive analysis and consideration of alternatives, we selected: _____

_____

    The main reason(s) we selected that alternative is because (decision rationale): _____

_____

_____

We expect the decision will result in (decision outcomes): _____

_____

Even the most experienced decision makers get it wrong sometimes. It is impossible to correctly anticipate all outcomes all the time. It is a reality that decisions made in ever-changing environments can cause unintended consequences. So, whenever possible, test your decisions (theories) before full-scale implementation. Learn as much as you can from the test and then apply what you have learned; it is a seasoned decision maker's rule. Finally, unexpected outcomes and unintended consequences are exacerbated by the multitude of relationships and interdependencies that exist in organizations. The more complex an organization, the more likely the unexpected or the unintended can occur. Focus on upstream and downstream interactions.

––––––––––––––––––––––

Well, this concludes *Competent Leadership*. I will close with how I started the book: *"Leadership applies to everyone, everywhere.* Whether a formal or informal leader, at work or at home, we all have to do it. It is not always planned, but when it happens, inevitably, someone has to step up. So, learning important leadership skills can only help. There is no downside." Share what you have learned; and since much of what we learned were life lessons, not just leadership lessons, it applies most everywhere to everyone.

ABOUT THE AUTHOR

T. S. (Steve) Marshall, Ph.D., is the founder and President of T. S. Marshall & Associates, Inc., based in Seattle, Washington. He has provided leadership and professional development training, consulting, and coaching services to employees in the U.S., Australia, England, Hong Kong, India, Indonesia, Philippines, Korea, Poland, and Singapore. Dr. Marshall's domestic and foreign travel, multicultural experiences, and personal relationships with people of many nationalities have resulted in substantial experience and expertise in leadership.